International Law Students Association

ILSA GUIDE
TO EDUCATION AND CAREER DEVELOPMENT
IN INTERNATIONAL LAW

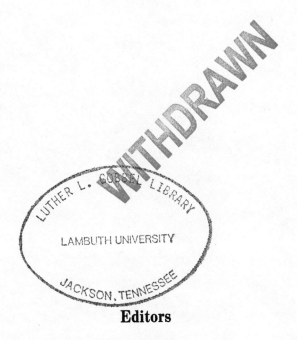

Editors

Jonathan Clark Green

Lafili & Van Crombrugghe,
Brussels, Belgium

Denise M. Hodge

International Law Students Association,
Washington, D.C., U.S.A.

Robert F. Kemp

Willian Brinks Olds Hofer Gilson & Lione,
Chicago, Illinois, U.S.A.

iii

ILSA GUIDE
TO EDUCATION AND CAREER
DEVELOPMENT
IN INTERNATIONAL LAW

Editors
Jonathan Clark Green
Denise M. Hodge
Robert F. Kemp

Associate Editor
Liz Heffernan

Assistant Editors
Marian Guinn
Lisa Hale
Robert Kramer
Arlene Zavocki

Research Assistants
Michael Dodd
Rachel Frank
Thea C. Michelet
Kerrie Murphy
Jeffrey Williams
Andrew Zovistoski

Administrative Assistant
Pamela M. Young

The entire ILSA community, especially those of us who have worked on this *Guide,* would like to express our most sincere personal regrets on the passing of Mr. George Gard of Western Newspaper Publishing Company. A friend to many of us and a strong supporter of ILSA activities, Mr. Gard played an important role in the early development of this *Guide.* His encouragement and unwavering commitment to international legal education through the written word will forever be appreciated and remembered.

INVITATION FOR COMMENTS

We have received assistance in this project from a great many individuals, not all of whom are listed on our masthead. Their contributions have added to the strength and diversity of this collective effort, and we are grateful to them for their help. Of course, any errors are solely our own.

As editors of the *Guide*, we realize that any effort of this magnitude will contain some errors and oversights. Every effort has been made to make this *Guide* as accurate and culturally and stylistically correct as possible. Still, we realize that errors are inevitable. Since we hope that this volume may be the first of a number of editions to follow over the years, we invite your comments, criticisms and suggestions for improvement. Later editions can only become better if we learn from our past mistakes, so please feel free to offer your thoughts. They will be greatly appreciated by future readers.

Denise M. Hodge*
On behalf of the Editors

* Fellow of the American Society of International Law and Executive Director of ILSA, Washington, D.C., U.S.A.; University of Denver (B.A. 1985), (J.D. 1988).

DEDICATION

This volume is dedicated to those individuals striving for the further study and practice of international law, with the belief that one day its greater implementation will lead to a world governed by the rule of law — the *sine qua non* of global peace.

J.C.G.
D.M.H.
R.F.K.

ILSA GUIDE TO EDUCATION AND CAREER DEVELOPMENT IN INTERNATIONAL LAW

TABLE OF CONTENTS

DIRECTORY OF SUMMER AND SEMESTER INTERNATIONAL AND COMPARATIVE LAW PROGRAMS WORLDWIDE

DIRECTORY OF ADVANCED DEGREE PROGRAMS IN INTERNATIONAL AND COMPARATIVE LAW WORLDWIDE

ILSA CONFERENCE OF INTERNATIONAL LAW JOURNALS

PHILIP C. JESSUP INTERNATIONAL LAW MOOT COURT COMPETITION

ILSA CONGRESS OF INTERNATIONAL LAW SOCIETIES

FOREWORD

The International Law Students Association

The International Law Students Association was founded in 1962 (under the name "Association of Student International Law Societies") by five international law societies, "believing that the principles of international law should be more fully understood and recognized" and "determined to educate ourselves and our fellow students in the principles of international law, international organizations and institutions, and the comparison of legal systems." In 1987, twenty-five years after its founding, the Association reconstituted itself as the International Law Students Association (ILSA), allowing for individual, as well as society, membership. An individual becomes a member of the Association by virtue of joining his or her local ILSA member society or, if no such society has yet been organized at the school, by direct application to the Association.

Membership in the Association at present includes international law societies and individuals at over two hundred law schools and law faculties throughout the world. These members are represented through the Association's Congress of International Law Societies, which meets at each Mid-Year and Annual Meeting of the Association. The Association's Mid-Year Meeting is held in the fall of each year, in New York City, in conjunction with the Annual Meeting of the American Branch of the International Law Association. The Association's Annual Meeting is held in the spring of each year, in conjunction with the Annual Meeting of the American Society of International Law (ASIL), usually in Washington, D.C.

The Association provides information and coordinative services for students interested in international law. Each year it co-sponsors the Philip C. Jessup International Law Moot Court Competition with the American Society of International Law. It also sponsors the Conference of International Law Journals.

The Philip C. Jessup International Law Moot Court Competition, founded in 1959, allows students of international law the opportunity to plead a hypothetical case, on a timely topic of international law, before a mock International Court of Justice. The participating teams, which annually represent approximately 250 universities and law faculties in forty countries on six continents, prepare written memorials (briefs) and present oral pleadings on

1

both sides of the dispute before three-judge panels. Regional competitions are held throughout the world from December through February. The International Rounds are held in conjunction with the Annual Meetings of the Association and the American Society of International Law in the spring.

The Conference of International Law Journals now consists of sixty-two student-edited international law journals from schools with ILSA member societies. The Conference annually hosts both a condensed workshop on international law journals at the Association's Mid-Year Meeting and a two-day conference during the Association's Annual Meeting, which includes panels, workshops and discussions on all aspects of running a student-edited international law journal.

In 1977, the Association began publishing the *ILSA Journal of International Law* (formerly the *ASILS International Law Journal*). The *ILSA Journal* is published once each year and is devoted exclusively to articles on timely subjects of international and comparative law, written by Association members. Each volume also contains the Jessup Competition materials from the corresponding year's Competition. Each year, the Association presents the **Dean Rusk Award**, to the author of the best article published in the *ILSA Journal*, and the **Francis O. Deak Award**, for the best student-authored article published in a student-edited international law journal.

Other Association publications include: the *ILSA Newsletter*, published four times a year; the *Handbook for Student International Law Societies*; the *Guide for Regional Administrators of the Philip C. Jessup International Law Moot Court Competition*; the *Philip C. Jessup International Law Moot Court Competition Reporter*; and the *Philip C. Jessup International Law Moot Court Competition Compendium*. The Association has also compiled an extensive list of speakers in the international law area for use by its member societies.

The *Philip C. Jessup International Law Moot Court Competition Reporter* and the *Philip C. Jessup International Law Moot Court Competition Compendium*, both of which are updated annually, are of special interest to Jessup teams. The *Jessup Competition Reporter*, designed as an annually supplemented looseleaf series, provides a detailed year-by-year review of Jessup Competition data from the first round of the Jessup in 1960 to the latest World Championship Jessup Cup Round, including, *inter alia*, the participation and performance of individual schools worldwide, the official results, and the recipients of the Best Oralist and Best Memorial Awards. The *Jessup Competition Compendium*, first published in 1981, contains the Jessup Problems, Judges' Memoranda, Official Rules, and Best Memorials from the Competition each year. In its present form, a full set consists of thirty hardcover volumes grouped by years from 1960 to the present.

The *ILSA International Law Citation Manual*, an authoritative text of citation forms for sources of international law, is an ongoing project of the Association. In addition, the Association has started an *International Law Video Lecture Series*, featuring the World Championship Jessup Cup Rounds of the annual Jessup Competition (since 1987) and substantive lectures on various topics in international law.

Individual membership in the Association is open to all students of international law. Society membership in the Association is open to international law societies, law faculties, graduate school organizations in international law and international relations, and internationally-oriented academic institutions, throughout the world, which meet the Association's constitutional requirements. Member societies and individual members of the Association receive the *ILSA Newsletter*, as well as the *Newsletter* of the American Society of International Law (ILSA's Host Professional Organization), and become a part of the ILSA worldwide network of information. Member societies also receive speakers lists and other relevant materials for society use. Membership and all other information may be obtained from the ILSA Executive Director, 2223 Massachusetts Avenue, N.W., Washington, D.C., 20008-2864, U.S.A. Telephone: 1-202-265-4375. Facsimile: 1-202-797-7133.

INTRODUCTION

General Comments

It is the dawn of a new age for attorneys worldwide, from the seasoned counsel for international business interests to the local family law specialist. The world has truly become one global marketplace, and its peoples a mosaic of interdependent, closely-linked groups. The fuel for this change, technology, with its 747's, microchips, facsimile machines, and supersonic transports, is expanding exponentially. Also expanding is the need for complete and competent international legal services.

International legal services, or "international law," as the term has come to be known in its most generic sense, consists of everything from state-to-state relations in international diplomacy, to purely municipal matters under municipal law, involving a party or element from outside the national jurisdiction. The common thread in all of these cases is the need for the traditional attorney to go beyond his or her domestic understanding of what constitutes law, procedure, and the cultural framework from which they come, in order to provide complete and competent legal counseling for the client, whether that client is a government, a businessman, or a family.

In many such matters, an understanding of international and foreign law, as well as conflict of laws, may be essential. But even if the law involved is purely domestic, an understanding of foreign systems of law and their cultural underpinnings may help to explain the actions of the foreign party involved and may even make or break what was otherwise a purely domestic negotiation.

The *ILSA Guide to Education and Career Development in International Law* is offered as a primer for all attorneys and prospective attorneys seeking to expand their understanding of international law, as well as their opportunities to practice it. For students, practicing attorneys and university professors alike, the *Guide* provides valuable information on entering the field.

The *Guide* can be divided into three main parts. The first part includes five essays which offer practical tips on entering the international legal field. Also included is a special feature, *What Makes A World Class Recruit—A Survey of International Law Firms*, in which various international law firms from around the world express their opinions about qualifications which they prefer in new recruits. The second part features two lists on educational

5

opportunities, one on special summer and semester programs in international law, and the other on master's and doctoral degree programs in the field. Finally, the third part provides information on student activities sponsored by ILSA, including the Conference of International Law Journals, the Philip C. Jessup International Law Moot Court Competition, and the Congress of International Law Societies. By reviewing these three parts in depth, the reader will gain a well-balanced and extensive body of information that should help enable him or her to successfully plan a rewarding career in international law.

Initiated in early 1987, the *Guide* is the culmination of the efforts of a host of individuals worldwide to compile a compendium of information on opportunities in international law. It is organized to provide a combined practical and academic guide for those wishing to enter the field.

Two other books from the United States concerning international law opportunities are available. The first, *Career Preparation and Opportunities in International Law*, [1] published by the American Bar Association, features a number of essays written by experienced individuals who discuss their respective areas of international law practice. It is an excellent narrative review of the various types of international law practice now available for the American attorney in particular, as well as the international practitioner in general. The second book, *Directory of Opportunities in International Law*, [2] published by the John Basset Moore Society of International Law of the University of Virginia School of Law, features the most complete and updated list of American law firms involved in international legal practice. The listings also include firms that have overseas branch offices. A commendable achievement, the University of Virginia publication provides a fine supplement of practical information for entering the field.

Both of these publications contain additional information that may prove highly useful for the prospective international attorney.

---

1. *Career Preparation and Opportunities in International Law* (second edition), John W. Williams, ed., American Bar Association, Chicago, 1985. This publication may be ordered through the American Bar Association, Order Fulfillment, 750 North Lake Shore Drive, Chicago, Illinois, 60611, U.S.A.

2. *Directory of Opportunities in International Law*, John Basset Moore Society of International Law, Charlottesville, Virginia, 1989. This publication may be ordered through the John Basset Moore Society of International Law, University of Virginia School of Law, Charlottesville, Virginia, 22901, U.S.A.

Therefore, it is recommended that they be used in conjunction with this *Guide*.

From whichever country you come, when using the *Guide* in mapping your strategy for entering the field of international law, you should pay special attention to four important areas that have traditionally contributed to successful career planning: information; education; experience; and, colleague/client development.

Information

By using this *Guide* in conjunction with the ABA and University of Virginia publications, you can find the basic information necessary to begin your quest for a position in the field of international law. Information, which on the international level is not always easily obtained, is, and always will be, an especially important part of planning any international legal career. International decisions, such as choosing an international law program abroad, are best made with time to spare. These decisions often involve traveling great distances and spending significant amounts of money. As a consequence, throughout your efforts in this swiftly developing field, you should continue to seek as much current information as possible.

Places to look for such information include professional international legal organizations and international sections of domestic legal organizations.[3] Many of these organizations publish newsletters

---

3. Following are some popular international legal organizations (and their main offices):

International Bar Association (London)
2 Harewood Place
Hanover Square
London W1R 9HB
UNITED KINGDOM

International Law Association (London)
Charles Clore House
17 Russell Square
London WC1B 5DR
UNITED KINGDOM
(over 40 branches worldwide)

Union Internationale des Avocats (Paris)
103, avenue Charles de Gaulle
92200 Neuilly-sur-Seine
FRANCE

Confederation Syndicale des Avocats (Paris)
34, rue Conde
75006 Paris
FRANCE

and journals and offer student membership at a reduced fee. In

World Jurist Association (Washington, D.C.)
1000 Connecticut Avenue, N.W.
Suite 202
Washington, D.C. 20036
U.S.A.
(composed of world associations of judges, lawyers, prosecutors, law professors and energy lawyers)

Association Internationale des Jeunes Avocats/International Young Lawyers
   Association (Brussels/Luxembourg)
c/o Me M.A. Bastin
avenue Louis LePoutre 59, Boîte 20
B-1060 Bruxelles
BELGIUM

The following are regional organizations with strong international membership:

The Arab Lawyers Union (Cairo)
13 Ittehad el
Mouhameen Fi
Arab St.
Garden City
Cairo
EGYPT

Asia-Pacific Lawyers Association (Seoul)
5th Floor
Korea Re-Insurance Building
80, Soosong-dong,
Chongro-ku,
Seoul
REPUBLIC OF KOREA
(Mailing address: KPO Box 354, Seoul, REPUBLIC OF KOREA)

Commonwealth Lawyers' Association (London)
c/o The Law Society
Law Society House
50 Chancery Lane
London WC2A 1SX
UNITED KINGDOM

International Jurist Organisation [Asia] (New Delhi)
C-12, South Extension,
Part One,
New Delhi 110 049
INDIA

Inter-Pacific Bar Association (Tokyo)
Secretariat
Nishiazabu Sonic Building,
3-2-12 Nishiazabu, Minato-ku,
Tokyo 106
JAPAN

addition, they and other private organizations often sponsor continuing legal education courses, seminars and special programs for international practitioners.[4] Two independent publications, the

---

LAWASIA [Law Association for Asia and the Pacific] (Perth)
C/-Law Society of Western Australia
GPO Box A35,
Perth, Western Australia 6000
AUSTRALIA

Union des Avocats Européens (Luxembourg)
31, Grand Rue
L-2012 Luxembourg
LUXEMBOURG

Inter-American Bar Association (Washington, D.C.)
1889 F Street, N.W.
Washington, D.C. 20006
U.S.A.

The following are other organizations with strong international membership:

American Society of International Law (Washington, D.C.)
2223 Massachusetts Avenue, N.W.
Washington, D.C. 20008-2864
U.S.A.
(Host Professional Organization for ILSA)

British Institute of International and Comparative Law (London)
17 Russell Square
London WC1B 5DR
UNITED KINGDOM

Section of International Law and Practice of the American Bar Association
(Washington, D.C.)
1800 M Street, N.W.
Suite 450
Washington, D.C. 20036-5886
U.S.A.

Please note that many jurisdictions have, in addition to the international sections of their domestic legal organizations, specialized organizations in international and foreign law on both the national and local levels. Examples of these in North America include the Canadian Council on International Law (Ottawa), the American Foreign Law Association (New York), the Washington Foreign Law Society (Washington, D.C.) and the Société Québécoise de Droit International (Montréal). For those holding a "foreign" law degree from a country other than that in which they practice, the Foreign Lawyers Forum (based in Washington, D.C., with chapters opening in other cities) may be of interest. For current information on these specialized organizations, contact the ILSA offices in Washington, D.C.

4. For a worldwide listing of continuing legal education courses, seminars and special programs for international practitioners sponsored by bar associations and other private entities, see *International Directory of Legal Seminars* (1985 edition), by Suzanne E. Engelberg (c/o the author, 518 Shasta Way, Mill Valley, California, 94941, U.S.A.). (*Note*: The 1985 edition is out of date. However, new editions are planned.)

International Lawyers' Newsletter[5] and the *International Financial Law Review*,[6] are also available. Published on a bi-monthly basis, the *International Lawyers' Newsletter* is a compilation of reports from offices located in North America, Asia and Europe. The *International Financial Law Review*, based in London, is published in magazine form on a monthly basis.

Other sources of information are professional law firm directories, such as the United States-based *Martindale-Hubbell Law Directory*,[7] which are published in a number of jurisdictions. Often, these directories will highlight a firm's speciality, such as "international business transactions," or list local corporations with international legal departments. The Section of International Law and Practice of the American Bar Association has released its own version of a specialized international law firm directory.[8] Chambers of commerce and foreign and economic ministries also publish such directories.

Yet another source of information is international law student organizations. Membership in the International Law Students Association (ILSA), or in another international law student organization, such as the European Law Students Association (ELSA) or the Australasian Law Students Association (ALSA), provides the international law student with a support network of activities, speakers, newsletters, and other publications specifically geared to his or her needs.[9] It should be noted that a number of universities around the world, although not yet members of one of these growing

---

5. *International Lawyers' Newsletter*, (bi-monthly), Kluwer Law and Taxation Publishers. This newsletter may be ordered through *International Lawyers' Newsletter*, Subscription Services, 101 Philip Drive, Norwell, Massachusetts, 02061, U.S.A.

6. *International Financial Law Review*, (monthly), Euromoney Publications PLC, London. This publication may be ordered through *International Financial Law Review*, Nestor House, Playhouse Yard, London, EC4V 5EX, UNITED KINGDOM.

7. *Martindale-Hubbell Law Directory*, (eight volumes; annual). This directory may be ordered through Martindale-Hubbell, Inc., P.O. Box 1001, Summit, New Jersey, 07901, U.S.A. A special international edition of the *Directory* is also available.

8. *ABA Guide to Foreign Law Firms*, Howard B. Hill and James R. Silkenat, eds., American Bar Association, 1988. This publication, or updated editions, may be ordered through the American Bar Association, Order Fulfillment, 750 North Lake Shore Drive, Chicago, Illinois, 60611, U.S.A.

9. For current information on these organizations, contact the ILSA offices in Washington, D.C.

organizations, are beginning to form their own local groups of students with a common interest in international legal practice. Seek out such groups, or form one yourself.

Two additional areas of potential information for the prospective international attorney include individual research and discussions with those presently working in the field. Individual research involves the continual reading of legal magazines, yearbooks, and journals in search of particular articles on international law opportunities and career preparation.[10] Books on related subjects are also available.[11] Finally, one of the best sources of information is that of attorneys who are presently engaged in international law practice. Whether on a personal level, during a conference, or even as part of an initial job interview, asking specific questions of those practicing in the field is always helpful. You should bear in mind, however, that times are changing, and what is true today may not apply in the years to come.

Education

The first step in planning a solid educational background in international law is choosing the right law school or university. Of

---

10. Three examples of such articles include "Special Feature: the State of International Legal Education in the United States," 29 *Harv. Int'l L.J.* 239 (1988); "Looking Toward the Third Millenium: The Practice of Transnational Business Law in the Year 2001," by Charles R. Irish, 2 *Transnat'l Law.* 1 (1989); and, of particular interest to African-American attorneys, "Debunking the Myth of International Law Practice," by Adonis E. Hoffman, NBA Magazine, Vol. 3, No. 5, p.18 (May 1989).

11. Examples of such books are listed below:

— *Lawyers in the European Community* (1988), available through the Office for Official Publications of the European Communities, 2, rue Mercier, L-2985 LUXEMBOURG, or through the offices of your local European Communities Delegation. (A review of EC Member State and Community-wide rules for the practice of law in the various EC Member States)

— *The Regulation of Foreign Lawyers* (third edition), by Sidney M. Cone III, American Bar Association, Chicago, Illinois, 1984. This publication may be ordered through the American Bar Association, Order Fulfillment, 750 North Lake Shore Drive, Chicago, Illinois, 60611, U.S.A. (A 1984 analysis of the regulations affecting foreign lawyers wishing to practice in the United States, as well as the regulations governing American lawyers wishing to practice in EC Member States and other foreign countries) (*Note*: Please check with the American Bar Association to see if updated editions are available.)

— *Transnational Legal Practice in the EEC and the United States*, by Linda S. Spedding, Transnational Publishers, Inc., Dobbs Ferry, New York, 1987. (A study of the freedom of movement among lawyers in the EEC and the United States)

course, many of us do not have a large number of choices of schools to attend, and, in some countries, there may be no choice. However, your initial legal education may be supplemented with outside courses or expanded by pursuing graduate courses in the field. Also, education in the field of international law goes well beyond course-work. Languages, travel experience, cultural awareness, and actual work experience are important parts of a well-rounded education in the area, as is a good background in related subjects, such as international politics and international economics.

If you do have a choice of which law school or university to attend, there are two approaches which are advised. The first is to enroll at the school with the best domestic law program, with little regard to the state of its international law program. Depending on the school you choose and your individual commitment to inter-national legal practice, this can work to your advantage. However, you should be cautioned that this is usually true only of those schools that enjoy a prestigious national or international reputation. If you must choose between what are often referred to as "second-" and "third-tier" schools, with varying local or regional reputations, you may be advised to follow the second approach. Using this approach, the extent of international law-related course offerings and overall support for the international law program should be given very se-rious consideration in your decision. There is, of course, no one way in which to choose a school. Whatever your choice, your individual commitment to an international legal practice will be the most im-portant factor in your future.

As stated earlier, whether the school you have chosen has a developed international law program or not, your education in the area can be supplemented by special summer, semester-long, or year-long programs. Such programs are usually located in foreign coun-tries, and offer an array of international law-related courses. These programs, a list of which is included in this *Guide*, are highly rec-ommended, especially if your school does not offer courses of this kind. For law students who do not have a traineeship, or "stage," period as a part of their legal education (e.g., American law stu-dents), it is also advisable to balance such special programs with as much practical experience during law school as possible, in order to enhance your marketability upon completing your studies.

There are two additional factors which you should consider in choosing a special program. First, you should ensure that your home school will accept the academic credit earned during the program if you wish to transfer such credit. Even though a program is recognized by a professional legal organization (e.g., the American Bar Association), there may still be some schools, regardless of their country of origin, which may be reluctant to accept such credit. Second, you should choose a program that most suits your educational needs, both inside and outside of the classroom. Choosing a program located in a country where you already have some language abilities and are familiar with the culture often allows you to develop further your knowledge and abilities to a level where they may enhance your marketability in this highly competitive field.

Another option is to enhance your international legal education by pursuing postgraduate study in the field. There may be some domestic law master's and doctoral degree programs in your home country in "internationally-involved" areas that offer such opportunities, such as taxation, trade legislation, intellectual property, and financial services. However, a number of fine master's and doctoral degree programs have developed in recent years, in many of the world's leading law schools and universities, that are specifically designed to provide the prospective international attorney with an excellent opportunity to expand his or her academic base in specialized areas of international law. An extensive list of such programs is included in this *Guide*.

These international law-related graduate programs vary from those devoted wholly to public international law, to those which consist of a general review of basic domestic law courses in a foreign legal jurisdiction. Whichever you choose, you should keep two considerations in mind.

First, if you choose a program involving comparative legal studies, it is advisable to select a program from not only another country, but also another legal system, or family of law. For instance, if you are a civil law attorney, choosing a program involving common law, Islamic law, or socialist law may prove more academically rewarding to you than a program involving civil law, and may increase your attractiveness for a job in the international legal market.

Second, regardless of the type of program you choose, it is often more enlightening and educationally rewarding to follow a program in a foreign jurisdiction. Not only do you have a chance to expand your cultural experience, and, perhaps, your language skills, but you also enjoy the opportunity to gain a different, broader perspective on a particular international law subject than you would by following the same program in your home jurisdiction. In addition, the unique opportunity to learn the particular subject along with your foreign colleagues will provide you with the hands-on experience of working directly with attorneys from foreign jurisdictions, which may prove very useful in your future practice.

Finally, extracurricular activities may play an important part in your academic development in the field of international law. Participating in international law moot court competitions, such as the Jessup Competition,[12] writing articles or editing an international law journal,[13] and being active in ILSA or other international law student groups,[14] are all excellent ways to expand your education in the field. Independent activities, such as foreign travel, attending cultural and religious events, or even enjoying foreign foods in a traditional ethnic restaurant, are also pleasant ways of obtaining valuable information which may be useful in working with clients in your future international legal practice.

Experience

Practical experience is perhaps the most important asset in finding initial employment in the field. This experience may be gained in various ways.

The first is through what is commonly referred to as clerking, articling, or doing a "stage" (or "traineeship") at a local firm in an area of domestic practice which interests you. Many areas of domestic practice, such as commercial contracts, intellectual property, or taxation, are easily transferrable to an international context. However, regardless of your area of domestic experience, practical knowledge of your own legal system and its customs of practice will prove invaluable in your future job search in the international arena.

---

12. Information concerning the worldwide Jessup Competition may be found in this *Guide*. Other regional international law moot court competitions currently operating include the following: the Telders Competition (Europe); the Concours Rousseau (French-speaking countries); the Commonwealth Competition (British Commonwealth); the Concours René Cassin (Europe/human rights law); the Southern African Competition (Southern Africa); the ALSA Competition (Australasia); the Niagara Competition (Canada-U.S.); and, the AEGEE Competition (Europe/European Community law).

13. A list of member journals of the ILSA Conference of International Law Journals is included in this *Guide*. Addresses are provided for authors seeking to submit articles.

14. Umbrella international law students groups currently operating include the following: the International Law Students Association (ILSA); the European Law Students Association (ELSA); the Australasian Law Students Association (ALSA); and, The Association des États Généraux des Étudiants Européens (AEGEE—European law student activities). For current information on these groups, contact the ILSA offices in Washington, D.C.

Many experienced international attorneys have said, "being a good international attorney begins with being a good domestic attorney." This is still most often the case.

As stated earlier, if you are from a jurisdiction where a "stage," or traineeship, is not formally required by the legal education system, it is very important that you obtain some practical experience, either domestic or international, during your period of studies.

Once you have gained some basic domestic experience in your home jurisdiction, it is advisable to supplement that experience with a traineeship of at least three months at a foreign law firm or legal organization. A foreign traineeship offers the opportunity to gain valuable, firsthand knowledge of a foreign legal jurisdiction and its customs of practice. Such an experience is especially important for those who plan to work with a particular foreign jurisdiction.[15]

A traineeship with a foreign firm involved in international practice is, of course, the most popular way of gaining such knowledge, for you can then contribute your own domestic experience to the activities of the firm. For those interested in multinational practice, working at an international firm is highly advisable because it can provide an excellent opportunity to experience foreign legal approaches to specific areas of international law practice, such as treaties, commercial contracts, conflict of laws, and international arbitration. As with educational programs, adopting a cross-system approach, where one does a traineeship at a firm in not only a foreign jurisdiction, but also a foreign legal system (or family of law), can be very enlightening and quite valuable in future practice.

Foreign legal traineeships are a recent phenomenon. A few law schools have provided such opportunities for their students over the past ten to fifteen years. Private programs have also developed.[16]

---

15. For those particularly interested in working as a foreign attorney in the United States, see the series of articles entitled, "Coming to America: So You Want to Work in a U.S. Law Firm?," by Laura Bocalandro and Monique van Herksen, beginning in the April 1990 *Newsletter* of the Foreign Lawyers Forum. For information on how to obtain these articles and other information on the Foreign Lawyers Forum, contact the ILSA offices in Washington, D.C. For those interested in working as a foreign attorney in Europe, see the article entitled, "So You Want to Practice Law in Europe?," by Frank L. Fine, in the Essays section of this *Guide*. For a general review of working as a foreign attorney in Asia, see the article entitled, "Go East, Young Lawyer," by Stephen W. Stein, also in the Essays section of this *Guide*.

16. Three of the largest private traineeship programs presently operating (and their main offices) are the following: the ILEX program of the Section of

However, it is only in the last five years that international law student groups have offered such opportunities on a wider scale. The most developed of these programs is the European Law Students Association's Short Term Exchange Program (STEP), which offers intra-European traineeships sponsored through ELSA's member national organizations.[17] ILSA, in cooperation with ELSA and other students groups, is now working to create a worldwide network for such traineeships.[18] Currently, it is possible for law students in some jurisdictions which require a "stage," or traineeship period, to spend a portion of that required period in a foreign jurisdiction.

Many large domestic law firms around the world are opening foreign offices or affiliating with (and, in some instances, purchasing) foreign law firms.[19] Working in such a domestic law firm may offer the possibility of working abroad for the firm after you have spent a certain period of time practicing in the firm's domestic offices. Policies concerning such "rotation" between domestic and foreign offices vary from law firm to law firm. It is advisable, therefore, to clarify the firm's policies in advance, as well as to confirm the types of law practice you may be exposed to in the firm's foreign offices, which also may vary.

An additional note is made here for those specifically interested in international business law. In-house legal departments of major corporations engaged in international business are becoming good training grounds for prospective international attorneys. In recent years, many of these legal departments have expanded their

---

International Law and Practice of the American Bar Association (Washington, D.C.); the University of the Pacific, McGeorge School of Law International Internship Program (Sacramento, California/Salzburg, Austria); and, the University of San Diego, Paris Institute on International and Comparative Law Clinical Internship Program (San Diego, California/Paris, France). Also, a number of study abroad programs have recently incorporated clinical internships into their curricula. For more information, see the Summer and Semester International and Comparative Law Programs section of this *Guide*.

17. For the current address of the ELSA Vice-President in charge of the STEP program, contact the ILSA offices in Washington, D.C.

18. For current information on the ILSA worldwide traineeship project, contact the Chairman of the ILSA Congress of International Law Societies, in care of the ILSA offices in Washington, D.C.

19. Recent American law firm activity provides an excellent example of this worldwide trend. As of January 1990, the following number of U.S. law firms have opened foreign offices, affiliated with local firms, or otherwise created a presence in the following cities: London 50; Tokyo 23; Brussels 23; Paris 19; Hong Kong 17; Riyadh 5; Amsterdam 3; Bangkok 3; and Sydney 3. Source: Hildebrandt, Inc.

overall activities to provide more competitive, lower-cost in-house legal services for their companies and to fulfill their companies' increasing demands in an era of international corporate expansion. This new phenomenon may now provide young attorneys with a viable alternative to traditional law firm or government legal training. Not only may working in such a department offer a greater chance of early international travel, it may also, depending on the department's activities, provide sufficient training for an attorney to be eligible for "lateral" hiring by law firms at a later date. This was not always true in the past.

Other ways of gaining practical experience in the field of international law include the following: becoming involved in international law-related projects of professional legal organizations; writing practitioner-oriented articles for international law journals; and, especially for those from jurisdictions unfamiliar with oral pleading-style appellate advocacy, participating in an international law moot court competition, such as the Jessup Competition.[20] Each of these activities can directly translate into practical experience which may prove valuable in your search for international legal employment.

Finally, there are some additional considerations that you should bear in mind if you are contemplating going abroad as a young attorney in order to develop an international practice. There are differing views about whether you should go abroad immediately after completing your legal studies or whether you should remain in your domestic jurisdiction, practicing and gaining experience in domestic law, before attempting to go abroad. There are advantages and disadvantages to each of these options. Your best choice depends upon your individual circumstances.

The following is an informal list of some of the advantages and disadvantages that may be involved in making such a decision:

Going abroad early - some possible advantages

- gaining exposure to foreign legal practice and customs at an early stage, perhaps with a more open mind;

- getting your name out and developing personal and professional relationships at an early stage for purposes of future client development;

---

20. *See* note 12, *supra.*

— gaining a better overview of future legal trends, the various opportunities available, and where your interests may lie, before mapping a long-term strategy;

— perfecting foreign language skills, including juridical terminology, at an early stage;

— opening the possibilities of an early overseas job opportunity that might not otherwise be available; and,

— gaining some foreign practical experience which may make you more marketable in your home jurisdiction.

Going abroad early - some possible disadvantages

— missing out on a regular interview season, possibly causing a delay in being hired upon your return;

— finding that you lack some specific domestic practical experience to contribute to a foreign firm, causing the firm to assign you more work on language-related activities than on legal activities (young U.S. attorneys should note here that an increasing number of foreign firms have U.S.-trained local attorneys in their offices, thereby reducing their need for assistance in matters involving basic U.S. legal skills);

— losing contact with colleagues in your home jurisdiction before being able to establish yourself on a professional basis;

— lost earnings, especially for those leaving a high legal fee jurisdiction for a lower legal fee jurisdiction;

— finding, upon your return, that some traditional domestic attorneys may question your commitment to practicing law in your home jurisdiction;

— creating additional financial obligations which may constrain your future choices of employment; and,

— forgoing some home jurisdiction opportunities due to age considerations.

Going abroad later - some possible advantages

— having solid domestic practical experience to offer for various job opportunities abroad, thereby increasing your marketability for such positions;

— having a domestic clientele and extensive colleague contacts in your home jurisdiction to offer a foreign firm doing, or seeking to do, business with your home jurisdiction;

- being in a much more stable financial condition to support your efforts;
- being more aware of domestic clients' needs with regard to international legal services, allowing a more focused approach to your efforts; and,
- increasing the possibility of working abroad sooner on a more permanent basis, if employed in the domestic office of an international firm that requires an associate to work for a certain period of time in his or her home jurisdiction before going abroad for the firm.

Going abroad later - some possible disadvantages

- forgoing any opportunity to go abroad due to future family, personal, or client obligations;
- finding yourself lacking foreign language skills at a late stage of practice;
- experiencing increased costs and possible career conflicts with a spouse due to relocation of family members;
- discovering that work abroad is not your true interest only after having left your established domestic practice; and,
- finding yourself more closed-minded with regard to foreign legal practice, while lacking knowledge of foreign legal trends and customs.

In addition to these general considerations of *when* to seek work abroad, there are also those of *where* to seek work abroad. As of the date of publication, the developing legal markets of the world (of varying sizes) that may offer new and unique opportunities to prospective international attorneys include Brussels, Berlin, Frankfurt (*am Main*), Vienna, Moscow, Budapest, Bangkok, Hong Kong, Singapore, Taipei, Tokyo, Los Angeles, and Mexico City. Of these, the most stable appear to be Brussels[21] and the Pacific Basin cities.

---

21. Since the entering into force of the Single European Act in 1987, Brussels has once again become a focus of international legal activity. A number of EC Member State firms, as well as non-Member State firms, have established new offices in Brussels. Most of these firms are seeking to capitalize on the perceived increase in the need for legal services caused by the opening of the internal European market in 1992. The actual extent of that increase, however, is disputed. Upon close examination, the Single European Act is, in reality, somewhat limited in scope, with most of its initiatives being implemented through domestic Member

However, these trends may be short-lived because they are subject to constantly changing political and economic factors of local, national, or international character. The best opportunities are still found in the world's traditional, established, large and medium-sized legal centers which are increasing their international orientation in order to meet the needs of modern society.

Three additional considerations that you should bear in mind concerning practicing law abroad are the process of registering as a foreign attorney in the foreign jurisdiction in which you wish to practice, the type of law you are allowed to practice there, and how you will be compensated for your services. Unlike general international business activities, law practice in most countries is a highly specialized, unique service that is strictly controlled by the government. There are often extensive government and local bar regulations regarding qualifications for practicing law, what type of law may be practiced (and by whom), and how legal fees are to be paid for services rendered. You must examine these conditions closely, as well as any local codes of professional conduct, before you begin to practice abroad.

An increasing number of jurisdictions around the world are allowing foreign attorneys to register (in varying forms) as foreign legal consultants. As such a consultant, you are normally subject to the local rules of professional conduct and are allowed to give advice

---

State legislation. Despite this uncertain demand for European legal services, however, many firms continue to invest in Brussels in anticipation of continued Community-level legal developments, often with their clients specifically requesting to be kept informed about the increasing activities of the EC Commission. This has created a legal environment which may provide new and unique opportunities for prospective international attorneys. At the same time, however, you should bear in mind that Brussels continues to be a much smaller international legal market than neighboring London or Paris. For those specifically interested in working at a law firm which practices European law in Brussels, extensive previous experience in the area, a special degree in European law, and/or completing a six-month "stage," or traineeship, at the Commission of the European Communities is highly recommended. It should be noted that, since 1988, obtaining a stage at the EC Commission has become highly competitive and increasingly difficult to realize without a personal, high-level recommendation, especially for law-related positions. In addition, spaces reserved for citizens of non-Member States are far more limited than those for citizens of Member States. For those who wish to do a stage at the EC Commission, early personal contact with officials, as well as multiple language abilities, are often essential. For a well-balanced and extensive article on the professional situation in Brussels, see "Brussels: Goldmine or Bandwagon?," Law Firm Supplement to *International Financial Law Review* (November 1989).

on international law and the laws of your home jurisdiction, but *not* on the laws of the registering jurisdiction. This registration, or licensing, of foreign legal consultants is often done on a reciprocal basis. For example, Belgium, Japan and the various states (*Länder*) of the Federal Republic of Germany only allow registration of United States attorneys who hold licenses from U.S. jurisdictions which grant similar, reciprocal registration to Belgian, Japanese and German attorneys, respectively. These U.S. jurisdictions include, *inter alia*, the States of New York and California, and the District of Columbia.[22] Therefore, if you are seeking to practice in a foreign jurisdiction, whether independently or on a "rotation" basis within a firm, be sure to obtain a law license from a jurisdiction which grants reciprocal registration to foreign attorneys, even if the licensing jurisdiction is not your place of primary practice. Otherwise, you may find yourself barred from practicing in some foreign jurisdictions which license foreign legal consultants.

Colleague/Client Development

Finally, the fourth area that has traditionally contributed to a solid strategy for entering the field of international law is colleague/client development. Throughout the process of collecting information and expanding your education and experience in the field, you should actively seek the acquaintance of others, both young and old, who share your interest in international law. Often referred to as "networking" or "making contacts," seeking acquaintances in the field is important for a number of reasons. These include finding those who may provide you with substantive support in specialized areas of practice; learning about additional job and educational opportunities; developing a future clientele; and, learning firsthand about the latest developments in the field.

One of the most obvious and effective ways to pursue colleague/client development is to become involved in the activities of both professional and student groups involved in international law. These groups range from international organizations for attorneys practicing international law,[23] to international law societies at local schools (which may be affiliated with a larger student group[24]).

---

22. As of December 1990, the other U.S. jurisdictions which license foreign legal consultants are the States of Alaska, Hawaii, Illinois, Michigan, New Jersey, Ohio and Texas.

23. *See* note 3, *supra*.

24. *See* note 14, *supra*.

Professional groups may even include non-law-related entities where those directly in need of international legal services gather, such as chambers of commerce, trade missions, or international trade associations.

Most of the organizations mentioned above have regularly scheduled meetings, conferences and seminars. Attend them when possible, and do not forget to bring a "carte de visite," or business card, no matter how temporary your situation may be. Whether for a future client referral, a job opportunity, or an exchange of information, such cards are invaluable assets to any prospective international attorney. It is advisable to provide a facsimile number on the card (if possible), to include complete country and city (area) codes in any telephone numbers on the card, and to keep an organized file for your own reference of the cards you receive from others.

Additional ways of pursuing colleague/client development in the area of international law include meeting and talking with people in the field while pursuing a foreign traineeship or program of studies; publishing an article or comment in a newsletter of one of the types of organizations mentioned above; participating on a panel at a meeting of such an organization; or, volunteering to judge at an international law moot court competition, such as the Jessup Competition.[25] In whichever activity you become involved, colleague/client development and the people you meet while pursuing it are among the most rewarding, enlightening and enjoyable aspects of any international legal career.

---

25. Judging at an international law moot court competition offers the prospective international attorney a number of opportunities. First, it provides an excellent continuing legal education course in public international law, which is becoming increasingly relevant in many international transactions. (At a 1989 meeting of the Section of International Law and Practice of the American Bar Association, the Jessup Competition was recognized as an excellent training program in international law for the Section's regular members, as well as for students of international law.) Second, judging at such a competition provides an unparalleled opportunity to meet and work with colleagues, both local and foreign, specifically involved in the field of international law, including senior partners from international law firms and government officials. In addition, participants in such competitions often pursue highly successful careers in the field in the years following their participation. The Friends of the Jessup, the professional support group for the Jessup Competition, drawn from the Jessup's nearly 30,000 former participants, judges and supporters worldwide, holds receptions and meetings in support of the Jessup Competition. Such receptions also offer an excellent opportunity to meet colleagues in the field. For more information on Friends of the Jessup activities, contact the Chairman of the Friends of the Jessup, in care of the ILSA offices in Washington, D.C.

Closing Comments

As stated earlier, these four important areas—information, education, experience and colleague/client development—have traditionally contributed to a successful strategy for entering the field of international law and should be considered when using this *Guide*. There is, of course, no one way of mapping a successful international legal career. Circumstances differ for each individual, and it will always be true that the luck of being "in the right place at the right time" may make all the difference in the world. However, you can improve your chances by being persistent, by exerting your best efforts, and, above all, by understanding the legal needs of the world in which we live.

The suggestions provided in this introduction are those of the author and do not necessarily reflect the views of ILSA or the ASIL. They are provided in the hope that they may assist you in your use of this *Guide* and in your efforts to pursue a successful career in international law. I would encourage all who read this *Guide* to become actively involved in the activities of ILSA and similar organizations and, in so doing, to contribute your suggestions and ideas on how we, as prospective international attorneys from around the world, can best meet the growing legal needs of our swiftly changing society.

Finally, I would like to extend my warm and personal thanks to ASIL President Peter D. Trooboff, ASIL Executive Director John Lawrence Hargrove, ILSA Chair Richard S. Alembik, and to those ILSA interns, ILSA staff members, members of the American Society of International Law, and Friends of the Jessup worldwide who made this *Guide* possible, especially Robert F. Kemp, Liz Heffernan, and Denise M. Hodge, my successor as the ILSA Executive Director. It is only through their many hours of often tedious work, as well as their personal encouragement, support and determination, that we are now able to offer this work to the benefit of our members and others in the international legal community. Congratulations on a job well done.

Jonathan Clark Green*
Brussels

---

* Member of the Illinois and District of Columbia Bars, U.S.A.; Visiting Attorney, Lafili & Van Crombrugghe, Brussels, Belgium; Fellow of the American Society of International Law and Executive Director of ILSA (formerly Executive Secretary, ASILS), Washington, D.C., U.S.A. (1986-1989); Columbia University (A.B. 1983); Illinois Institute of Technology, Chicago-Kent College of Law (J.D. 1986).

PREFACE TO THE
ESSAYS ON OPPORTUNITIES
IN INTERNATIONAL LAW

The following is a collection of essays written by experienced attorneys in the field of international law, in which they express their views on pursuing a career in the field. The views expressed in these essays are those of the authors and do not necessarily reflect the views of ILSA or the ASIL.

If, after reading these essays and the introduction to this *Guide*, you sense that there are a number of divergent views on how to pursue a career in international law, then you will have a good understanding of the situation. In fact, there are a number of differing opinions and perspectives on the issue, with no one view articulating the "ideal" career path applicable to all prospective international attorneys.

Differing types of practice, your personal circumstances, and your individual will to forge ahead in searching for your own niche in international practice will all affect these choices. In choosing your path, remember that many, including those of us affiliated with ILSA, believe that the journey to finding your place in international law can itself be a highly rewarding experience.

TO BE AN INTERNATIONAL LAWYER:
AN ESSAY

*by John W. Williams**

To be an international lawyer, you must first be a good lawyer. The practice of international law, especially private international law, is highly competitive. The demand for jobs is still greater than the supply of such openings. This means that, in order to enter the field, you must excel in law school. There is no more fundamental advice I can give than this.

The practice of international law falls into two general categories: public international law and private international law. The former includes human rights and public interest law. The latter, also referred to as transnational law or international business law, is the main focus of this *Guide*. It is also where the greatest interest is and where the greatest financial reward is.

In the briefest terms, private international law is the practice of domestic law (corporations, contracts, commercial law, torts, etc.) across international boundaries. The scores of different jurisdictions compound the conflict of laws problems, while the cultural differences compound the personal and professional relationships.

Even though the world economy appears to be growing, the number of attorneys practicing international law full-time has not increased dramatically. Yet, the financial rewards and the "sexy" aura of the practice attract a lot of interest among law students. This means that the field is still highly competitive.

The initial level of competition is to obtain that first position with a law firm or corporation which practices international law. Every law student already knows the challenges of the competition for that first job—grade point average, class standing, law review, Order of the Coif, interviews, resumes and clerkships.

It is redundant to recite the sage advice given to all law students about how to get ahead in law school. A survey of the former chairmen of the American Bar Association's Section of International Law and Practice, conducted several years ago, revealed that the advice holds true for the aspiring international lawyer.

---

* John W. Williams is an attorney and an assistant professor at Principia College in Elsah, Illinois, U.S.A. He is the editor of *Career Preparation and Opportunities in International Law*, published by the Section of International Law and Practice of the American Bar Association, and the producer of a videotape entitled, "International Legal Research," in the ILSA *International Law Video Lecture Series*.

Many of the chairmen, themselves senior partners or corporate counsel involved in international practice, admitted that they did not view the study of international law as a necessary criterion for employment. They also indicated that advanced law degrees, such as an LL.M. in international law, were not necessary. However, they acknowledged that the study of international law was useful preparation for an international career. More importantly, it signifies that the law student is really interested in the subject.

The chairmen also noted that the command of a second language is useful and might help set one candidate for a job above another. They cautioned, however, that English is still growing in popularity as *the* international business language.

The struggle to practice international law does not end with initial employment. The competition continues within the law firm or corporation. It often seems that international law is the province of the partners, or at least of the most senior associates. This means partaking in the constant struggle within the firm to enter international practice. A few firms have also been known to endure battles among partners.

One of the recurring themes in articles discussing the attributes of international practice is the foreign branch office. In most instances, the American lawyer will be in a small branch office. This may mean more autonomy in decision-making, but it may also mean a more general practice, since there will be fewer attorneys to handle a broad array of legal matters. And it may mean less support from colleagues. In effect, the American practicing abroad is on the front lines. According to one attorney who was interviewed, "you're pretty much on your own."

There is a perception among associates that practice in a foreign branch may actually be a detriment to their careers. One article aptly questioned, "Are lawyers abroad victims of the 'out of sight, out of mind' syndrome?" The author concluded otherwise: "Indeed, associates who have checked their firms' records before taking a foreign assignment unanimously report that a higher percentage of past associates with overseas experience have made partner over those without that experience." If this is true, the competition for international experience will heighten as associates scramble to advance their careers.

A small number of adventuresome attorneys have started their own solo or small practices in international law. In almost all cases, these attorneys have been able to develop contacts or have a special skill (such as command of a foreign language and foreign legal systems) or special expertise (such as technology transfer or customs law). It requires special initiative to overcome all of the inherent barriers to solo practice and to international practice. Nevertheless, these attorneys have proven it is possible.

A growing number of attorneys are finding that their domestic legal practices are expanding to include international matters. The "trickle-down" theory of international law is evident in the growing number of state and local bar activities and committees involved in international law. There are also more "part-time" international lawyers attending American Bar Association activities.

Unfortunately, the practice of international law is not as exciting as it sounds. For the United States-based attorney, after the first couple of trips abroad, international travel can quickly lose its appeal. (You may as well be flying into the Holiday Inn at Chicago's O'Hare International Airport.) As with other areas of practice, international law can slip into a dull routine. This is, in part, because international law is as much a forum for the practice of more usual types of municipal law as it is its own body of law.

The foreign-based attorney is away from family and familiar surroundings. For single attorneys, a foreign culture can be exciting. However, families, especially young ones, can find foreign living difficult. There are also professional problems with overseas practice. First, the attorney may risk losing contact with trends in domestic law. He or she may drift out of touch with peers and superiors.

Despite my admonitions, I recommend the practice of international law. There are several practical steps one can take to learn more about a career in international law and to prepare for it. For more information about the practice of international law, I recommend *Career Preparation and Opportunities in International Law*, published by the Section of International Law and Practice of the American Bar Association. It is an excellent companion to this *Guide*. The ABA monograph is a conceptual approach rather than an analytical approach to the nature of international legal careers.

As a law student, there are a number of valuable steps you can take to further your international career possibilities. First, you should join a professional organization, such as the American Society of International Law, or the ABA's Section of International Law and Practice. This will be the first step to developing a professional network of contacts as well as scores of great personal friendships. "Networking" is an essential tool in obtaining employment and in furthering one's law practice once it is underway. Both organizations welcome student involvement and participation. The latter organization, the ABA Section of International Law and Practice, is the largest professional organization of private international lawyers in the United States. You should not overlook smaller or specialized groups, such as the International Business Law Association or the Washington Foreign Trade Law Association. Most state and large local bar associations have international law committees.

There are two law school activities that focus on international law, and are well understood in the employment process — law review and moot court. There are dozens of student-edited and managed international law journals. They are growing in number and respect. As with a law review, membership on an international law journal, editorship, and publication of a note, carry weight in the hiring process.

International law is the subject of one of the most prestigious moot court competitions in the world — the Philip C. Jessup International Law Moot Court Competition, cosponsored by the International Law Students Association and the American Society of International Law. Many younger international lawyers were on Jessup teams and many senior international lawyers have served as judges.

As the survey of former chairmen of the ABA Section of International Law and Practice revealed, advanced degrees in international law, study abroad programs, prior international experience and command of a second language are not essential prerequisites for international legal practice. In themselves, they will not enhance a weak academic record. On the other hand, such experiences and qualifications indicate a strong interest in international law and may help to prepare a young lawyer for international practice.

Any student who thinks he or she is interested in international law should, at a minimum, join the law school's international law society. He or she should also take a basic course in international business law or international legal transactions. A basic public international law course may be a prerequisite. The risk of taking this prerequisite, however, is that you may discover an interest in public international law, a field that desperately needs lawyers.

Although the practice of international law is competitive, there are opportunities available. One must begin to prepare during law school, by becoming as involved in the school's international legal studies program as possible. There are several schools which have comprehensive international programs. Some also offer joint master's degree programs in international relations and M.B.A. programs in international management. For more information, you should contact the schools in which you are interested.

Perhaps the strongest attribute you must have to enter the practice of international law is persistence. You must have the requisite qualifications, but you must also be willing to continually strive toward the ultimate goal of securing one of the scarce international positions.

"I WANT TO BE AN INTERNATIONAL LAWYER"

by *Joseph P. Griffin**

Having just completed the current round of hiring season interviews, my partners and I were struck by the large number of
interviewees who said, "I want to be an international lawyer." Usually when I ask these interviewees what they mean by that statement I receive vague responses having to do with travel, working
with treaties and public international law issues. The responses are
often colored by the particular classes the interviewee took in law
school. I well remember when I was a law student interviewing for
my first job and made the same statement to the senior partner of
a distinguished law firm. His reply was, "There's no such thing as
international law, there's only the practice of American law for clients with funny sounding names." I doubt that the same response
would be given today. Nevertheless, there is undoubtedly a fair
amount of confusion about what many members of our Section [the
Section of International Law and Practice of the American Bar
Association] do to earn a living. The following is addressed to our
1,500 law student members and other younger members. It represents one man's attempt to offer an explanation of what an
"international lawyer" does.

Perhaps the best place to start is to look at our Section's
Directory. We have divided ourselves into four Divisions. The
General Division handles administrative and publication matters and
is not relevant to this discussion. The other three Divisions, Business
Law, Comparative Law and Public International Law, represent our
attempt to subdivide the general topic of "International Law and
Practice" into rational subtopics. The Public International Law
Division covers those areas devoted to relations among nations, the
law of treaties, international human rights and other classic public
international law topics. The Comparative Law Division focuses on
comparisons between U.S. law and the law of particular foreign
countries or regions. The Business Law Division addresses a number
of topics related to the application of U.S. law abroad or the

---

* Joseph P. Griffin is a past Chairman of the Section of International Law
and Practice of the American Bar Association.

application of U.S. law to foreigners doing business in the United States.

One of the things that attracted me to our Section and to international practice in general is its variety and breadth. The growing list of Committees within the Section reflects, to a large extent, the richness and diversity of the work of its members. More than one senior official of the American Bar Association has told me that our Section covers nearly all aspects of American law. That observation accurately reflects the fact that the special knowledge and experience of the international law practitioner typically overlaps with the substantive and procedural expertise usually associated with other fields of law. This seems to be borne out by the fact that many other ABA Sections have international committees.

An international practitioner may be principally a litigator, a deal-maker, a regulatory expert, or another type of legal specialist. What distinguishes the international practitioner, however, is a familiarity with bodies of information, techniques and strategies that relate to the solution of legal problems that cut across national borders; involve foreign languages, laws and customs; or relate to the special treatment accorded under U.S. law to non-U.S. persons in this country, or to U.S. persons abroad. If a person practices international tax law it is really a matter of self-image whether he believes he is a tax lawyer who happens to practice international law, or an international lawyer who happens to practice tax law. In either case, that lawyer is going to have a breadth of experience and a discernible expertise that sets him apart from his peers who specialize in domestic tax law.

For several years the Section has published a book entitled, *Career Preparation and Opportunities in International Law*, which is now in its second edition. It contains a wealth of information directed to law students, answering often-asked questions about international practice on such matters as planning for a career in international law, practice with the federal government, private corporations and non-profits. I recommend that book to any student interested in entering the field of international law.

Among those applicants I have interviewed for positions with the international section of my law firm, those who have made the greatest impression on me share three common attributes. First, a strong academic record including evidence of ability to write well and do competent legal research. Second, a personal resumé that reflects a familiarity with foreign cultures and languages, and a sensitivity to the kinds of special issues and concerns that an international lawyer deals with. Finally, an entrepreneurial spirit. As international practice continues to evolve and expand into new areas, those new lawyers who possess these attributes are likely to find themselves at the forefront of the field.

GOING GLOBAL: BIG LAW FIRMS
EXPAND OVERSEAS

by *Timothy Harper* *

James A. Kiernan III was worried. As managing partner in the Paris office of Debevoise & Plimpton, the 314-lawyer Manhattan law firm, he had made sure everything was finally in place on both sides of the Atlantic for a client's multibillion-dollar corporate takeover.

Almost everything, that is. A certificate from a Dutch accountant that would allow $700 million to be moved back to the States still had not come in on the day the deal was supposed to close. And the Dutch accountant who was supposed to file the certificate had disappeared from his firm's Rotterdam office.

Where was he? Hundreds of people—lawyers, bankers, investors, accountants, corporate executives—were waiting in dozens of offices around the world. Was the deal, after months of building an intricately interrelated financing, tax and legal structure in several countries, going to come tumbling down like a house of cards? "I couldn't believe it," Kiernan recalled.

Finally, three hours later, Kiernan found the missing accountant; he had for some reason decided to drive from Rotterdam to the accounting firm's office in Belgium. Kiernan gave the accountant half an hour to file the certificate by telefax. He did it, the $700 million was transferred to the States and the takeover was completed minutes ahead of the deadline.

For Kiernan, it was just another day of international law practice. Obscure legal requirements, huge sums and even temporarily missing Dutch accountants are part and parcel of the increasingly lucrative and increasingly competitive world of global law practice.

While a few small law firms and sole practitioners have always carved out cross-border specialties, it is becoming common—many say necessary—for big U.S. firms to open foreign offices and to build up their legal expertise in international law. From the traditional foreign legal centers such as London and Paris, in the last decade

---

* Timothy Harper is a London-based American journalist and lawyer who writes on international politics and economics.

American law firms have stretched themselves from Hong Kong and Tokyo and Sydney to Moscow and Stockholm.

"Globalized law practice is definitely a trend," said attorney Peter Cleary. "It's largely because of the globalization of business." Cleary is a partner in the Tokyo office of Coudert Brothers, historically one of the most foreign-minded New York firms and the first to open in both Beijing (1979) and Moscow (1988).

Indeed, many American companies increasingly rely on their overseas operations for their profits. Colgate-Palmolive, for instance, sells more than half its toothpaste and soap outside the United States. Naturally, as U.S. corporations expand abroad, they demand more legal services abroad, and their existing law firms are eager to give it to them. They follow their clients, and they follow their clients' transactions; as Citibank expanded in Europe, Asia and the Middle East, its longtime New York law firm, Shearman & Sterling, expanded its offices to Paris, London, Hong Kong, Abu Dhabi and elsewhere.

The big firms, however, do not usually go overseas just to keep their existing clients. They're looking for new business, too—especially in the rapidly growing financial services sector. The era of merger mania has helped make the practice of law more "transactional" in nature. The corporations and investment banks involved in buyouts or in need of any type of creative corporate finance are often less interested in establishing lasting relationships with any one firm than in retaining whatever firm promises to do the best job on the particular deal at hand.

If a deal has a European aspect, a client may be more likely to choose a firm that already has a European presence.

"To effectively service the financial markets, a firm needs offices in each of the three world financial centers: New York, Tokyo and London," Cleary said. "You can make the same argument for fields such as mergers and acquisitions. A lot of the techniques developed in a sophisticated community like New York are being exported."

In this atmosphere of global competition for clients, law firms are not limiting themselves to helping American clients make deals abroad; they also pave the way into the States for foreigners, and play a pivotal role in exporting innovative U.S. financing techniques to Europe and Asia. They make alliances with foreign law firms not only to gain the local expertise, but also in hopes of gaining referrals when those foreign firms' clients look do to business in the States.

So far there have been two paths to globalization: Baker & McKenzie's, and everyone else's. Baker & McKenzie is the Chicago-based firm that has 1,300 lawyers (including 430 partners) spread over 39 cities in 22 countries. But many other big American law firms aren't even sure Baker & McKenzie qualifies as a "firm" in the same way they do.

Many of Baker & McKenzie's foreign branches, for example, were acquisitions of local law offices rather than true expansions of the firm's American lawyers, and many of those foreign branches typically operate with more legal, financial and management independence than the offices opened abroad by other firms.

Instead, most of the several dozen big firms with overseas offices use their own homegrown talent to staff those outposts. The emphasis is on keeping the branches integrated into both the firm's day-to-day operations and its long-term culture. Few foreign jurisdictions allow lawyers from American firms to practice that country's law, even if they have dual qualifications. And some countries, notably Japan, have thrown up some considerable obstacles that discourage U.S. law firms from setting up branches to advise on American law.

Japan did not allow American law firms in at all until 1987, and under restrictions that seemed to be aimed at protecting Japan's small, closed legal community. For example, a firm cannot be set up under its own name; rather it must use the name of the managing partner. Consequently, Cleary does not technically work for Coudert Brothers in Tokyo. Instead, he works for the Charles R. Stevens Foreign Law Consultancy Service. If and when Coudert partner Charlie Stevens returns to New York, Coudert Brothers has to go through the bureaucratic paperwork of changing its name to the name of the new managing partner.

But it probably won't be Cleary. Japanese authorities are insisting that he leave the country because he does not meet another technical requirement: that foreign lawyers in Japan have at least five years' experience in their home jurisdictions. Cleary, admitted to the bar in New York, only practiced in Coudert's main office for three years before spending seven years doing international law in the firm's Hong Kong office. But because the Japanese don't recognize those seven years, he has been denied working papers in Tokyo.

"The five-year rule really works to deter younger lawyers from coming to Japan," Cleary said. "Typically, young associates interested in Japan want to come over after two or three years in New

York. If they have to wait until their sixth year, they're often reluctant to make a move. Though it's not an issue in our firm, some
people feel uneasy about being away during their last years as an
associate, when partnership decisions are being made. The Japanese
rule penalizes international experience."

Besides the difficulties of getting into some countries, there are
many stumbling blocks to the nuts and bolts of practicing abroad.
"One of the big problems is that American-style documentation is
usually very long and detailed," Cleary said. "That's not the way
it is in most Asian countries. In China, the approach is to be short
and vague—except for the exact amount of money each side will
kick in. You often have to fight tooth and nail to get details into
a contract, and the Chinese are extremely hostile to any use of foreign law."

A number of countries, however, are in the process of making
it easier for American law firms to provide services in their jurisdictions—a trend that is sure to hasten the coming of the truly
"global" practice of law. Foremost among these countries is Great
Britain, where Prime Minister Margaret Thatcher's government has
proposed sweeping changes in the British legal system. One of the
key changes would allow English solicitors to work in multinational
partnerships: merged U.S.-U.K. law firms of American lawyers and
English solicitors, in other words.

In anticipation of that change, which still requires approval from
Parliament, O'Melveny & Myers, the Los Angeles firm, announced
a "strategic alliance" with Macfarlanes, the London solicitors. The
two firms said they will keep separate managing partnerships, but
intend to work together on various projects, share client representation and perhaps set up joint offices together in other European
countries.

Bruce Buck, managing partner in the London office of New
York's Skadden, Arps, Slate, Meagher & Flom, said he believes there
will be a full-fledged merger between American and British law firms
within the next two to five years. A big part of the reason, he said,
is the increasing competition among law firms at home, the satu-
ration of legal services and the growing problems of conflict of interest.

American firms need new clients, and they can find them in
Europe.

"The large American law firms have to look to the international arena as a growth area," he said. "Because of conflicts of interest, they can never have more than a certain percentage of the
market in the United States."

Buck, noting that American firms account for 55 of the 90 foreign law firms with branches in London, said his firm and most other
big American firms have several options: to open more branches of
their own in European capitals such as Frankfurt, Milan and Madrid; to make alliances with local law firms; or to undertake an outright merger with a European law firm.

European expansion is especially significant these days because of 1992. That's the date the 12-nation European Community
has set for bringing down all its internal trade barriers and creating
a true single marketplace. Instead of conforming to 12 different sets
of technical requirements for everything from manufacturing to
shipping, a company can gain access to one EC country and auto-
matically gain access to the other nations.

The opportunities for cashing in on what promises to be the
world's richest consumer market have led to a flurry of reposition-
ing and restructuring among European companies, along with a
European expansion rush by many big companies from non-EC
countries, especially the United States and Japan, to make sure they
have what Buck called "a foot in the door."

"There's a lot of fear of Fortress Europe," Buck said. "If you
want to grow, and most companies do, you've got to have a foot in
both markets, North America and Europe. For American law firms,
the fields of management buyouts and leveraged buyouts are heav-
ily populated. There are a lot of people who want to do those transactions. And since there are a lot of European countries following
those strategies because of 1992, law firms are taking their American
experience and trying to adapt it to the European marketplace."

Dovetailing the 1992 drive with the globalization of law practice, some American firms with branches overseas are actively re-
cruiting lawyers with dual qualifications. Debevoise & Plimpton, for
example, opened its London office early this year with five lawyers,
including one, Linda O'Shea Farren, who is also qualified as a solicitor in Ireland. Under the EC's 1992 rules, lawyers from one EC
country will be able to undertake some types of practice in the other
11 countries. In theory, Farren could represent the firm's American
clients in local European courts.

Besides exporting the financial market techniques developed in
the United States in the 1980s — takeovers (friendly or hostile), management buyouts, new share offers, divestitures, borrowings, etc. —
U.S. law firms are finding that they can go abroad to develop new
techniques applicable back home. The case of the missing Dutch
accountant is a good example in that it involved the takeover of one

American corporation by another, but Debevoise & Plimpton devised a way of using foreign subsidies to help finance the deal.

In early 1988, Black & Decker made a $1.8 billion takeover bid for American Standard, the New York-based bathroom fixtures company whose subsidiaries include WABCO, the brake manufacturers, and Trane, which makes commercial air conditioning systems. Black & Decker subsequently increased its bid to $2.1 billion, but American Standard didn't think that was enough and threw itself open to better offers. One came from Kelso, the New York investment banking firm, for $2.5 billion. That offer was accepted, provided Debevoise & Plimpton, Kelso's lawyers, could figure out a way to arrange the financing, including $1.6 billion of debt.

Kiernan flew in from Paris and presided over a month of brainstorming sessions that finally resulted in a novel plan that took advantage of American Standard's heavy overseas presence (more than half its $127 million net income was from non-U.S. operations).

Instead of raising all the money in the States, Debevoise and Plimpton decided to place $875 million of the debt on existing American Standard subsidiaries in Canada, West Germany and Britain. A new Dutch subsidiary also was created just for the deal. Kiernan and Edward Perell, then based in New York but now the managing partner in charge of the new Debevoise & Plimpton office in London, drafted a detailed memo outlining the plan. The memo, circulated to banks, helped nail down the necessary bank commitments.

Then the paperwork really began. The European debt angle was handled from the Paris office of Debevoise & Plimpton where, Kiernan recalled, "We had four telefax machines going 24 hours a day."

"One of the most difficult parts of a deal like this is getting the foreign-borrowed money back to the States," Perell said. Working with Canadian, West German, British and Dutch lawyers and accountants, Perell and Kiernan devised a way not only to get the money back, but to get it back without having to pay the usual taxes.

After the Dutch accountant's certificate had been received by fax and passed on by fax, the deal was finally closed—also by fax. That shows how important modern communications are to global law practice. "It would have been impossible to do this deal without telefax," Kiernan said. And, of course, without a certain Dutch accountant.

SO YOU WANT TO PRACTICE LAW IN EUROPE?

*by Frank L. Fine**

When I was a student at Loyola Law School in Los Angeles
in the early 1980s, a small group of us had the idea of becoming
international lawyers. We were working for *The International and
Comparative Law Journal*, which, at the time, had a definite leaning
toward Europe. Our office walls were covered with posters of rug-
ged Alpine peaks and quaint cobblestone passages. A number of my
fellow staff members would come back from their summer vacations
with wonderful stories about the Alps and the rickety, narrow
streets. Though the real money was supposedly in the Orient, I sat
there, I'm sure, in wide-eyed enchantment with Europe. Once in a
while, I spoke on the phone with some of our contributors on the
Continent, which somehow made Europe, a place which I had never
seen, that much more magical and seductive.

Several years later—in 1986 to be exact—my feet fortunately
touched the ground, but they did so in Brussels, Belgium. I've been
there ever since.

If you have had the thought of living and practicing law in
Europe, whatever you do, don't dismiss it as an idle fantasy. There
is a way. The "Foreign Section" of the *Martindale-Hubbell Directory*
will attest to that. Unfortunately, however, the means are not all
too clear. I'll try to give you the benefit of my own experience.

Needless to say, living in Europe is nothing like hopscotching
on a Eurail pass. If you have the right motivation and background,
practice in Europe can be incredibly challenging, rewarding and fun.
You could be involved in a broad spectrum of commercial practice
or in the burgeoning field of European Economic Community (EEC)
law, which has an impact on everything from customs law to pack-
aging, labeling, and distribution. You will learn and apply the laws
of a number of countries in a multitude of different transactions. If
you are working in Brussels or Paris, you will inevitably have to
read and speak French. You will develop contacts with other U.S.
and European lawyers operating in this highly specialized market,

---

* Frank L. Fine is an attorney with the Brussels, Belgium, office of Frere
Cholmeley.

many of whom will become colleagues and friends. You will also have the challenge of being pushed immediately onto the firing line, as you will not be one of legions of young associates in the office. Law firms in Europe tend to be much smaller than their U.S. counterparts.

The social advantages are equally interesting and obvious. There is nothing quite like having all of Europe as your backyard. (I know one associate for a U.S. firm in London who manages to fly somewhere almost every weekend.)

So you ask — or should be asking — what is the downside? First, there is the culture shock. Believe it or not, whether you are in England or on the Continent, the native population will not have quite the same outlook as you, even if you think you identify with the local culture. The disparity of perspective, on an indefinite and daily basis, can be disquieting, but, after time, you can overcome it. Additionally, if you are not in an English-speaking country, you had better be functional in the native language or you will be spending many lonely nights listening to Armed Forces Radio. You will also have to deal with foreign taxation, foreign landlords (many of whom think that the pockets of Americans are lined with gold), and the lack of a number of items you take for granted (no Mexican food or NFL football, to name a few).

Then there is the matter of work hours. Don't expect to be strolling down the Champs-Elysées at 6 in the evening. Most European and U.S. law firms operate on the old pyramid structure, which means longer hours for the associates. (One of my friends, an associate for the Brussels office of a New York firm, is in the office until 10 or 11 almost every weeknight.)

Last but not least, there is the issue of money. Salaries in Europe are, in general, lower than those in the U.S., and the legal profession is no exception.

How can you prepare yourself academically for a job in Europe? Two items are virtually indispensable: a solid grounding in at least one foreign language (preferably French or German) and a course in EEC law. Courses in comparative law and conflict of laws are also helpful. If you can publish a European-flavored law review article, become an editor of an international law journal, or spend a semester in a European law school, so much the better. The thing to remember is that your potential employer will be looking primarily for evidence of commitment to European practice. The second axiom to remember is one you have already learned: there is no substitute for experience.

Now to the nitty-gritty: how to nail down the job. I would propose to you four rules of thumb:

1. You must plan a trip to Europe for the sole purpose of seeking a job;
2. You should use the resources available to you;
3. You should network as much as possible; and,
4. You should stay away from the Wall Street firms.

YOUR TRIP TO EUROPE

If you expect to find a job in Europe by staying in Los Angeles or Cleveland or Dallas, don't waste your time reading this article. You must be in Europe for the simple reason that nobody will fly you there for the interview. (I might also add that all serious applicants find a way to go.) So how do you arrange your European tour? There are actually three ways to do it.

The first and least effective means is the one which requires the least effort. You grab *Martindale-Hubbell*, send resumes to all of the firms which interest you, and let them know when you are coming. You will then have to follow up all of your letters with telephone calls to confirm receipt which is really a pretext for establishing contact. Since you can make this European tour during your vacation, it really involves the least risk and shows the least sign of commitment. You can expect the senior partner to question whether you are prepared to live in Europe, particularly if you have no prior academic or work experience in Europe. Try to understand the predicament. Many Americans who think that they will enjoy the expatriate life sour on it in less than a year.

The second means of setting up your European visit is much more effective. It is a little-known fact in the States that Americans may obtain paid internships ("stages") with the European Commission in Brussels. As a lawyer, you can work in the European equivalent of the U.S. Justice Department (the "Legal Service") or in its antitrust division ("Directorate General IV"). During the six months you are there, you will see how the Commission, the nerve center of the EEC, runs from the inside. European law firms understandably view this experience as something akin to a stint with the Treasury Department or the SEC in the States. Since the internships are high prestige items in Europe, the competition for them is extremely keen. Your advantage is that few Americans know about the internships. The pay may be rock-bottom, but if you are able to get the stage, you will be instantly marketable.

The third way to get to Europe is easier to arrange than a stage with the Commission, but is less likely to result in a job offer. Floods of young U.S. lawyers have discovered that an LL.M. at a European university can provide the springboard that they need to land a European job. Applications at such places as Cambridge, Oxford (which has a two-year B.C.L.), and the University of London, have skyrocketed in recent years. You can obtain a great deal of useful knowledge in an LL.M. program, particularly in civil law (which is the law of most of Europe) and EEC law (which is in force in twelve European countries). During your stay, you will not only get an idea of whether you wish to remain more permanently, you will also demonstrate staying power to potential employers. The only real drawback is, of course, that you are gaining still more academic rather than hands-on experience.

Nonetheless, I can tell you from my own experience that an LL.M. program can be very productive. A word of advice: if you choose this route, be aware that most of your competitors are already onto "Oxbridge." If you are lucky enough to get into one of these elite English universities, you may have as many as fifteen fellow American lawyers as classmates, each of whom is equally as qualified as you and as hungry for a job in Europe. A viable alternative is the Vrije Universiteit Brussel, which provides an LL.M. course in English. Or, if you want a workout in French, you can try the College of Europe in Bruges or the University of Paris. Each of these continental universities is well respected and represented in the law firms on the continent. With the unfavorable exchange rates, tuition and living expenses will cost you much more than you would have paid several years ago. But on the other hand, even nine months spent in places like Cambridge or Oxford will cost you much less than you would pay for an LL.M. at Harvard or Georgetown.

A final word on arranging your trip to Europe. Whether you simply come for two or three weeks, do the "stage" at the Commission, or enroll in an LL.M. program, do not be duped by the charms of Europe. Stories abound of errant American lawyers who arrive in Cambridge, muddleheaded and gooey-eyed, and proceed to blow nine months in private dinner parties and fox hunts. Don't fall for it. You are in Europe to work. When holidays and vacations roll around, take advantage of them by taking quick hops to other capitals. See people—they won't come to you. If you luck out and find a job, you'll have many opportunities to smell the flowers in Kew Gardens.

YOUR RESOURCES

You will discover quickly that the *Martindale-Hubbell Directory* is your best friend. If you get on the plane without having photo-copied the listings for the cities which interest you, you may not have another chance when you arrive. Aside from a few law firms, virtually no one carries *Martindale* in Europe. If you do find one in a university library, it is likely to be too old and dusty to do you much good.

After *Martindale*, your available resources drop off fast. If you have followed this quest for very long, you've undoubtedly been advised to read the Tuesday edition of the *London Times* and the Thursday edition of the *Financial Times*, in which there are employment ads for lawyers. Unless you plan to buy these papers for other reasons, you could better spend your money on a Cadbury bar. About 99 percent of the lawyer ads in these papers are for English solicitors. Even when the ad is placed by companies like Chevron or Wang, it will almost always state that it seeks applications from solicitors. This means that applications from U.S. attorneys will not be seriously considered. Another piece of misleading advice is that concerning the London headhunters. Yes, there are many of them, and a number of them specialize in legal employment. But again, their predominant interest is in placing barristers and solicitors.

In my view, aside from *Martindale*, your most useful source of information will be the lawyers you contact in Europe. This means that you will have to network.

ON NETWORKING

As an American seeking work in Europe, it may not dawn on you that, despite your competition, you will be considered to be a different kettle of fish. The fact is that most U.S. lawyers are perfectly happy earning better money in the States. Since you are different, and without the resources that you would have at home to assist you in your search, many lawyers, in both U.S. and European law firms, will be more than willing to talk with you. If you fail to obtain leads on existing job openings, you should at least walk out of the interview with an idea of which firms hire Americans.

ON WALL STREET FIRMS/ALTERNATIVES

Many of the U.S. law firms with European offices are large Wall Street or D.C. firms. True, their associates in Europe are paid high U.S. salaries and are generally treated like royalty. But be wary. Their associates are almost always hired in the States and sent to Europe for a one- or two-year rotation. (Interestingly, a few of them jump ship when they are in Europe for something more permanent.)

Thread the needle if you dare, but remember that aside from your competition with the hordes in New York or D.C., you must also be one of the lucky few to receive the European carrot.

Your best chance for permanent employment in Europe is with the U.S. law firms based in Europe. You will find them scattered between London, Brussels, Paris, and even Italy. As your next best bet, I would suggest the local law firms in Brussels. You will find that the Brussels bar is very lenient in permitting American lawyers to affiliate with local attorneys. Evidently, London-based law firms are also opening their doors somewhat to U.S. lawyers.

With the weakening dollar, U.S. companies are already increasing their exports to Europe. This could result in an increase in available legal positions. To hearten you in your research, I'll leave you with a short sketch which appeared in the *International Lawyers' Newsletter* in 1984 on a prominent L.A. lawyer, Harry Donkers, who sold his partnership interest in a prosperous downtown firm in order to practice solo in Paris. Maybe this will inspire you, as much as it did me.

"As you get older, time gets shorter. You have to be true to your inner drives. There are certain things that you can't NOT do. If you don't do them, you'll be regretful."

Strolling down the Boulevard de Courcelles to grab a morning espresso in the local cafe, Donkers is clearly not regretful of the chance he took in 1978.

GO EAST, YOUNG LAWYER

U.S. Legal Services Hot New Export to Asia

*Stephen W. Stein**

Some years ago Russell Baker suggested in *The New York Times* that many of the nation's economic problems could be solved if the United States would trade some of its lawyers for some of Japan's engineers. I wonder today if Mr. Baker might reconsider his jest, given that American legal services are becoming a "hot" export not only to Japan, but throughout the Pacific Rim and Asia.

Approximately 15 American law firms have now opened offices in Tokyo under the new Foreign Lawyers Legal Consultants Act. In addition, there are 16 U.S. law firms in Hong Kong and five with branch offices in Singapore. Although the earnings of these foreign offices will hardly be noticed in U.S. trade statistics, the trend clearly is toward overseas expansion at a rapid rate.

In light of this, we should ask ourselves if American legal services are indeed a promising export—or whether we are rushing headlong down the same path as many corporations that encountered unexpected obstacles when competing overseas.

For legal services, the outlook is very promising. The role of the American lawyer is uniquely suited to the particular needs of Asian business and finance. In fact, it seems clear that the American law firms which succeed in Asia will be in a position to dominate this giant market.

There are three basic reasons why American legal services are thriving in Asia. One relates to the documentation of business transactions; a second has to do with process—the actual negotiation of the deal; and the third is language.

Traditionally in Asia contractual relationships are based on the "handshake" concept and the personal relationships between the parties involved. Guidelines for conduct are left intentionally ambiguous to allow for adaptation of the transaction to changing conditions.

---

* Stephen W. Stein is a partner at the New York law firm of Kelly, Drye & Warren. He specializes in international and Pacific Rim practice.

U.S. practice, for the most part, differs substantially. Contracts tend to be lengthy and complex in an effort to anticipate as many eventualities as possible and to provide for resolution of these issues within the text. Great emphasis in American legal education and practice is placed on the ability to draft documentation for complex transactions.

In the early postwar period, when American business dominated international transactions, these American contracting practices were imposed upon Asian parties, either through economic leverage or on the premise that these practices were "standard." Even today we find relatively little training, know-how or experience among Asian lawyers in structuring complex, sophisticated contracts (although their expertise is sure to increase over time).

But Asian parties have become more involved in international transactions, fueling a demand for expertise to assist in negotiating these types of contracts. By sheer numbers and experience, the American legal profession tends to dominate international transactions — except those intimately involving the United Kingdom or Australia.

American lawyers are also valued for their negotiating skills. Generally speaking, Asians resolve issues by consensus; confrontation is usually avoided. This approach complicates the negotiation of an intricately detailed transnational agreement, which requires the expeditious development and resolution of many specific issues prior to contract execution.

American lawyers are trained and experienced in an adversarial system where confrontation is expected and can be accommodated without creating an uncomfortable atmosphere. Although Asian parties are certainly as competent as any others to negotiate the economic and business substance of a transaction, they are disadvantaged in the negotiation of the documentation. Authoritarian and hierarchical traditions in some Asian countries may further complicate the negotiating process by inhibiting flexibility and responsiveness as well as the internal decision-making process.

The American lawyer can bridge this gap in the Asian client's experience or expertise.

With the growing recognition in Asia that legal counsel must be introduced at an early stage in a negotiation, American lawyers enjoy another advantage. Asian lawyers are usually litigators and not advisers; not surprisingly, they have a limited capacity to serve in the latter fashion. In fact, it is often considered impolite to have lawyers attend negotiations.

The American lawyer, on the other hand, has been acting as counselor to clients for many years. Certain Japanese clients particularly seem to value the "business judgment" of American lawyers and distinguish this type of advice from purely legal advice. In addition, the American lawyer's willingness and ability to work out the mechanics of a transaction is seen as a valuable tool which is not always otherwise readily available.

Finally, English is the language of international business transactions in Asia. Here, American lawyers (and, of course, their British and Australian counterparts) have a great advantage over practitioners in the Asian countries, many of whom speak English as a second language. This is particularly so because many of the nuances of complex transactions are not always easy to express other than in English.

The opportunities for American law firms in Asia go far beyond servicing foreign clients in relations with U.S. companies and the United States. Financial, commercial and trade transactions are increasing between Asian countries and countries outside of Asia other than the United States.

Contractual models used in these transactions, for the most part, will be those developed in trade and business with the United States. The language of these contracts in most cases will be English. The concepts will be those that have been developed in trade with the Untied States and other major industrial countries. There will be a definite need for U.S. legal talent in this area.

Of course, competition in Asia is already stiff, and will increase as more U.S. firms attempt to establish or maintain branch offices in the Pacific Basin.

The successful firms will be those that recognize the personal nature of business relationships in Asia and the need to understand the political, economic, social and cultural context of the transactions in which they are involved. This will require that American lawyers receive more education and training in the backgrounds of these countries and conduct longer tours of duty in overseas offices. There will be a greater need for commitment to training lawyers who will spend their professional careers in this environment.

For those firms that are willing and able to make this commitment, Asia represents a ready and rewarding market.

WHAT MAKES A WORLD CLASS RECRUIT —
A SURVEY OF INTERNATIONAL LAW FIRMS

INTRODUCTION

What should an aspiring international lawyer do to prepare for a career in the private practice of international law abroad? The underlying objective of this survey is to offer insights to those individuals who are seeking a foreign assignment and who are preparing for a career in the private practice of international law.

Many law students and recent law graduates, such as myself, have considered careers in international law, and it is natural to seek out the most complete source of information on the subject. The foremost work still remains *Career Preparation and Opportunities in International Law* (John W. Williams, editor), published by the Section of International Law and Practice of the American Bar Association. Yet this publication, despite its diversity and depth, lacks the broad input of international practitioners that this survey seeks to provide. The nature of the private practice of international law abroad is so rich and varied that a single essay on the subject is insufficient. This survey offers the reader an opportunity to glean a variety of perspectives from several different sources: American branch offices abroad; sole practitioners overseas (both American and foreign) who regularly handle international legal problems; and, large foreign firms with significant international practices.

The impetus for this survey came after I had spent my second year of law school on a fellowship in international law with an American law school program in London and had worked for two firms abroad, one a foreign firm, the other a branch office of an American firm. Coincidentally, I clerked for an American law firm in London at the same time as the American Bar Association held its annual meeting there. At the ABA conference, I had a chance to meet many international lawyers and quickly learned that the private practice of international law abroad was quite diverse. I was anxious to know how I could learn more about the opportunities that were available in international law and what the best preparation would be for a career abroad. Thus, the concept of an international law survey began.

I started the project during my third year of law school with an initial mailing to about one hundred firms abroad. After learning that there were several important firms I had overlooked in my first mailing, I circulated a second survey to another one hundred law firms overseas. After searching for an outlet for publication and editorial assistance in preparing the survey in its final form, the project is now complete. Although some time has elapsed since the compilation of this data, I believe this survey still offers valuable insights into the private practice of international law abroad.

Admittedly, putting together a profile of the "ideal candidate" for a career abroad in the private practice of international law is not an easy task. Soliciting advice from attorneys who practice in the international arena can be a frustrating experience. The reason is not because international practitioners are unwilling to share their expertise. In fact, as the results indicate, quite the opposite is true. Those who practice international law recognize the eclectic nature of the practice and are quite willing to offer advice to others who will follow in the profession.

The difficulty lies in the nature of a written survey. Copies of the survey were sent to over two hundred law firms in several countries around the world. The response rate was about thirty percent. In addition to the obvious problem of sending an unsolicited survey by mail to lawyers abroad, the survey itself is not statistically random, which means that it is quite unlike the nature of most polling data in its reliability. Instead, the results are qualitative in nature, offering anecdotes and advice to those who are interested in pursuing this kind of practice. Also, the questions were posed from the perspective of a United States law school graduate, and therefore may not be as applicable to young lawyers from other countries. (I would argue, however, that the results would be similar for foreign lawyers wishing to practice with American firms abroad, since the skills American firms seek in their attorneys are generally the same.)

With this last point in mind, I apologize for the use of the terms "abroad," "foreign," and "overseas" to any non-United States law students and lawyers who may read this survey. Given the background of the author and the primary audience, the terms are appropriate. Also, all responses have been converted into American English for use in this text. Still, I hope you will find that the advice contained in this survey is universal to all those who have an interest in learning more about the private practice of international law.

More problematic, perhaps, is the definition of what makes a lawyer "international." Many American attorneys based in the United States meet the "international" requirement by having foreign clients. Most lawyers based abroad are "international" due to their geographic location, and because, quite often, foreign clients are involved and foreign lawyers are consulted. In this latter scenario, foreign legal systems come into play and knowledge of cultural and language differences add to the legal equation. Clearly, the definition of what makes an "international lawyer" varies widely. I will leave the precise definition of what constitutes "international law" to others, but suffice it to say that the respondents to this survey considered themselves to have such a practice.

Ideally, you should come away from this survey with some sense of what those who work in the field think is valuable vis-à-vis career preparation for private practice. Given the changing nature of international business, however, by the time some readers reach the stage of their careers when they have a truly international practice, the field may have changed dramatically and, therefore, the advice contained in the survey may prove to be less valuable. Still, it is unlikely that any other candidate would be better prepared than those who follow the advice offered by those currently working in the area.

Readers who take the advice contained in this survey to heart should realize that the nature of the respondents varies. Some respondents are resident partners with hiring power, others are associates in branch offices overseas who are serving a "rotation" abroad (usually without hiring power), and still others are with foreign law firms that would likely not be interested in hiring an American lawyer, save one with exceptional cultural/language/legal skills. You should also note the number of responses for each country, as frequency of response obviously should be a measure of the weight to attach to the advice offered. With this background, it is important to weigh the offered advice against your own interests and strengths.

Finally, many of the respondents requested that their names and/or the names of their firms not be used for publication.

Given that the purpose of this survey is to offer an overview of the private practice of international law abroad and not intended as advice as to how to prepare to work for any one firm, this was easily accommodated.

The importance of international practice is no doubt growing as the ever-changing international business environment continues to evolve. Firms in the forefront of such a practice will certainly prosper as they stand ready with personnel trained to meet the changing demands of their clients' international legal problems. Law students and recent law graduates alike can certainly profit from taking advantage of the advice contained in this survey as they prepare for the challenges that lie ahead in the private practice of international law.

Robert F. Kemp*
Chicago

ACKNOWLEDGMENTS

The author wishes to thank the following individuals for their encouragement and assistance in the preparation, circulation and editing of this survey: Nancy Kemp DuCharme; Jonathan Clark Green, Liz Heffernan, Denise M. Hodge and Pamela M. Young of the International Law Students Association; Mr. and Mrs. William J. Kemp, Sr.; Mr. and Mrs. Robert J. Rasmussen; and, John W. Williams of Principia College.

---

* Associate, Willian Brinks Olds Hofer Gilson & Lione, Chicago, Illinois, U.S.A.; Court Law Clerk, United States Court of Appeals for the Seventh Circuit (1987-1989); Columbia University (A.B. 1982); University of California at Berkeley (J.D. 1986); Northwestern University (M.S.J. 1987); The John Marshall Law School (LL.M. 1990); The University of Chicago (M.B.A. 1990).

FRANCE

Number of Respondents: *23*

Firm Description

1. Is your office a branch office of a firm? If yes, where is the "home" office of your firm?

Fifteen out of twenty-three respondents indicated that they are with branch offices of a firm. Over half of these stated that their home office is located in New York City. Two respondents have their home offices in London, and two in Mexico City. One firm is based in Washington, D.C., and another in Paris.

2. With which countries does your firm do the most significant amount of business?

Over half of those questioned singled out the United States as the country with which they conduct most of their business. These respondents are both French and American firms. Similarly, a majority of respondents stated that a significant amount of business centers around France itself, while one-third look upon the United Kingdom as a major source of business.

A number of firms deal with other European countries. For example, five respondents do business with Belgium, four with Germany, three with Italy, and three with Switzerland. Another seven firms indicated that they deal with Western European countries in general.

Although only a small number of respondents referred to other sources of business, the variety of countries mentioned is worth noting. Five firms conduct business with Japan, and three with French-speaking African countries. Dealings with South America, the Middle East, the Far East, Australia, and New Zealand were listed by just one or two firms in each case.

3. How many lawyers are there in your office?[1]

Two-thirds of those questioned stated that there are less than ten lawyers in their respective offices. Interestingly, most of the remaining offices (which all house more than ten lawyers) are branch offices of foreign-based firms. Two American firms, with

---

1. This question may have different responses throughout the survey, depending upon how the respondents interpreted the question. While most respondents listed the number of lawyers in their respective offices as the "local" number, some may have opted to include the firm-wide total.

home offices in New York City, employ twenty-six and forty-five lawyers, respectively, in Paris. In both cases, however, American lawyers are in a minority in the Paris branch office.

The respondents employing the least number of lawyers (between one and five) are made up of both French firms and branch offices of either international or American firms. The largest French-based firm among the respondents employs fourteen lawyers.

4.   In which areas of the law does your firm practice the most?

Overall, the responses revealed a wide variety of practice areas among the respondents. In no case is a single area of practice common to all or even to an overwhelming majority of those questioned.

Joint ventures and licensing agreements were most frequently listed, with over two-thirds of the respondents indicating that these areas provide substantial business. A majority of firms referred to international taxation as an area of concentration, while just under half mentioned banking law, corporate law, EEC law and transfers of technology.

Roughly one-third of the respondents conduct a significant practice in the following areas: antitrust law, conflict of laws, debt restructuring, intellectual property law, and mergers and acquisitions. One-quarter of the firms specialize in international arbitration and labor law, while a small number practice in areas of French domestic law.

Professional Qualifications

5.   Which state bar examinations would be of the most value for a young lawyer to pass? (For example, are most of your American transactions conducted under New York or California law, etc.?)

The vast majority of respondents (both French and American firms) consider membership in the New York state bar to be the most valuable. Six out of twenty-three firms also value membership in the California state bar. Two French firms would favor a French qualification in a job candidate. Similarly, a Mexican qualification is preferred by firms based in Mexico City, and membership in the District of Columbia bar by a firm which has its home office in Washington, D.C.

6.   How important is it to your firm that your attorneys understand foreign legal systems?

A majority of firms consider an understanding of foreign legal systems to be very important. Only four of the firms questioned, however, described it as a prerequisite. One New York attorney stated: "For us, the French language and a general understanding of civil law are the key elements we look for."

7. Are there members of your firm who are qualified in more than one country? If yes, does this dual qualification make a job applicant to your firm significantly more attractive to your firm?

Twenty out of twenty-three respondents stated that lawyers in their firms are qualified in more than one jurisdiction. However, only half of these firms are of the opinion that a dual qualification significantly enhances job candidacy with their firm.

8. If your firm is located in England, Hong Kong, or Singapore, would qualifying as a barrister in England increase your interest in a job applicant, assuming that this individual was already qualified as an American lawyer?

The overwhelming majority of respondents did not consider this question to be applicable to them. Only one firm (which is based in London) was prepared to endorse this additional qualification, although two other firms suggested that it might be a helpful asset.

9. If your firm is located in France, would earning a D.E.S.S. degree from the Université de Paris (I) increase your interest in a job applicant, assuming this individual was already qualified as an American lawyer?

Half of those questioned stated that this qualification would significantly increase their interest in a job applicant. However, one-quarter of the respondents rejected it outright. The remaining responses suggested that it might be of some value, but only as an additional factor. Notably, a small number of French firms considered that a different French qualification might be more appropriate (e.g., a basic French law degree, or *conseil juridique* qualification).[2]

10. Do the lawyers in your office seek or accept locally-generated business?

All of the offices questioned undertake locally-generated business.

11. Is dual nationality an important consideration in your hiring?

The majority consider dual nationality to be an important consideration. In France, membership in the local bar (as an *avocat*) is limited to French nationals.[3]

---

2. *See* note 4, *infra.*
3. *See* note 4, *infra.*

12. Is it difficult to obtain a work permit for foreign lawyers in the country where your firm is located?

Most respondents did not envision any difficulty in acquiring a work permit for a foreign lawyer. Indeed, some were of the opinion that no work permit is necessary. Others emphasized that EEC nationals are at an advantage, and that foreign lawyers from non-EEC countries may encounter difficulties. One American firm indicated that the process of transferring an individual from their New York office to their Paris branch office does not present any problems.

13. Is it difficult for foreign lawyers to become members of the local bar?

A majority of the respondents indicated that there is some difficulty in this regard. Many noted that since membership in the bar is limited to French nationals, it is impossible for a foreign lawyer to practice as an *avocat*. One French lawyer explained: "In France, the bar is separated; foreign lawyers are admitted as *conseil juridique* and restricted in practice, i.e., with respect to local law."[4]

Educational Requirements

14. In general, would you advise a student coming out of law school, who wished to practice private international law, to qualify in a foreign jurisdiction, obtain an LL.M. in a specialty area, or go into practice with a large multinational firm?

A number of firms recommended more than one of the options listed. Most firms advocated going into practice with a large

---

4. Since this survey was completed, new restrictions have been put in place limiting the ability of non-French lawyers to practice law in France. *See* the amendments modifying the Law of 31 December 1971, in the *Journal Officiel* of 5 January 1991, pp. 219-229. These amendments eliminate the classification of *conseil juridique* and require all lawyers to have the full qualifications of an *avocat* in order to practice law in France. These changes are subject to certain exceptions for citizens of EC Member States and other jurisdictions which provide reciprocity for French lawyers. The exceptions, which often involve special exams, are promulgated on a case-by-case basis in the *décrets d'application* adopted by the French Ministry of Justice. (For copies of the relevant materials, contact the offices of the *Journal Officiel*, 26, rue Desaix, 75015 Paris, FRANCE, or the Ministère de la Justice, 13, place Vendôme, 75001 Paris, FRANCE.) For further information on the effects of the change in the law on American attorneys, see, *e.g.*, "New Law to Affect U.S. Lawyers Practicing in France," *Chicago Daily Law Bulletin*, 27 December 1990, p. 1 (copies available from the Law Bulletin Publishing Company, 415 North State Street, Chicago, Illinois, 60610, U.S.A.).

multinational firm. One French lawyer stated: "My preference is for practice with a multinational law firm, or in a good law department of a multinational corporation, especially in a foreign location and with extensive foreign travel." An American attorney recommended "practice with a large or medium U.S.-based firm having a significant international practice (corporate, financial, commercial, trade law)." He emphasized the importance for an American lawyer to have practiced in the United States prior to going overseas, "since the U.S. legal, analytical approach is useful and difficult to obtain in smaller overseas offices which are less well-equipped to train young lawyers." A number of respondents tended to favor prior specialized work experience in a job candidate. For example, an international firm specializing in maritime law insists on prior exposure to that specialty area.

One-third of the respondents recommended that a student leaving law school qualify in a foreign jurisdiction. One-third also advocated acquiring a specialty LL.M. degree. One respondent in an international firm stated: "I'd recommend that the student get a first-class legal education, and then start practice in a U.S. firm, if possible, in an overseas office."

15. Does your firm value highly any of the following experiences for aspiring international legal practitioners? If so, why?
— LL.M. degree from an American law school in a specialty area that lends itself to international work (e.g., tax)
— LL.M. degree from a foreign university, preferably from a law school in the jurisdiction in which he/she hopes to practice in the future (e.g., EEC law, intellectual property law, international business transactions)
— M.B.A. in international business
— Clerkships[5]
— Government experience[6]

Two-thirds of the respondents place significant value on graduate degrees. The LL.M. degree from a foreign university is

---

5. The following clerkships were listed individually, and should be applied to responses to Question 15 throughout the survey: U.S. Court of International Trade (trade law); U.S. Court of Appeals for the Federal Circuit (intellectual property law); U.S. Tax Court (tax law); U.S. federal circuit courts of appeals; U.S. federal district courts; and, state supreme courts of the United States.

6. The following government positions were listed individually, and should be applied to Question 15 throughout the survey: Office of the United States Trade Representative; U.S. Department of Commerce (Office of Legal Counsel); U.S. Department of State (Office of Legal Counsel); and, the International Trade Commission of the United States.

the most popular among the respondents, with fourteen out of twenty-three firms endorsing it. Ten firms value the LL.M. degree from an American law school, and seven firms prefer an M.B.A. in international business.

Only seven firms view clerkship experience as having significant value, and five of these firms are American. For some, the type of clerkship is not important: "We generally like clerks (high quality students and lawyers usually), but have no preference as to where they clerk." A French lawyer commented: "Foreign experience is of the first importance — any clerkship is impressive. We prefer hands-on experience in practicing *and* living in a foreign country to additional educational credentials."

One American attorney warned that aspiring international lawyers "should be made to recognize that working in a sophisticated international environment requires special preparation and very specific skills .... it is pointless to apply if one does not possess them."

Cultural Skills

16. **What qualities would your firm wish to see in the ideal candidate? That is, what kind of educational background and cultural skills should the ideal candidate possess?**

The responses revealed a wide range of qualities listed by the various firms. The single most popular attribute is a proficiency in languages. Thirteen out of twenty-three respondents value language skills highly. Many describe their ideal candidate as bilingual, and a small number of firms would favor a job candidate who has spent some of his/her childhood in the cultural setting.

Nine out of twenty-three firms look for a strong academic background in their ideal candidate. One French firm recommends "a formal education in civil and common law, plus a fair degree of specialization one way or another, in a specific area of the law." A small number of firms suggested that a background in business or accounting would be useful, while others prefer a liberal arts background.

Most firms value some form of prior cultural experience or travel. For some, however, prior work experience is of greater importance. An American attorney explained: "For American lawyers, we look for individuals who have demonstrated abilities by practicing in our New York office. Knowledge of the French language is useful." Another respondent recommended "a solid law school background, focus on corporate, tax, and commercial law, followed by at least 2-3 years of U.S. practice in a firm with international work."

Other qualities were mentioned by some respondents, such as adaptability, communication skills, and what one respondent described as being "culturally well-rounded." One international lawyer expressed his view in these words: "The ideal candidate has the puritan work ethic, high integrity, and a sense of cultural relativity, with a love of the French language and people."

17. How much does your firm value prior experience in a culture (e.g., time spent there during Junior Year Abroad, Summer School programs during college and law school, prior work experience, or travel)?

Roughly half of the respondents place significant value on prior cultural experience. The remainder either declined to comment, or alternatively suggested that such experience is merely an accessory. One respondent suggested that the experiences listed above are "helpful, but less than a normal living experience." A small number of firms consider prior work experience in the cultural setting to be of the greatest value.

18. How many years of prior domestic practice would you recommend as a prerequisite to a young American lawyer before embarking on an international practice in a foreign jurisdiction?

On average, three years of prior domestic practice was recommended. A small number of responses favored either less than three years, or between three and five years. One American attorney emphasized the importance of prior domestic practice, stating that candidates who would practice initially overseas may be doing themselves a disservice: "...they cannot realistically hold themselves out as American lawyers (if they have never practiced in the U.S.), which is often what our European clients hire us for, i.e., our U.S. style, rigor, analysis, and organizational and drafting skills."

19. How much value do you place on language skills for applicants for an attorney position with your firm?

An overwhelming majority value language skills highly. Of these, roughly one-third consider such skills to be a prerequisite.

20. Which languages do you value most for your attorneys?

Out of twenty-three firms, twenty value French, and twelve English. Eight respondents listed German, and six mentioned

Spanish. Italian, Japanese and Arabic are each of value to just one or two respondents who conduct business in countries using those languages.

HONG KONG

Number of Respondents: 5

Firm Description

1. Is your office a branch office of a firm? If yes, where is the "home" office of your firm?

Three out of five offices questioned stated that they are branch offices of a firm. In each case, the home office of the firm is located in the United States. Two of the firms are based in New York City, and the third firm in Chicago, Illinois.

2.   With which countries does your firm do the most significant amount of business?

There was a broad spectrum of responses to this question, with most of the respondents stating at the outset that their international clients are many and varied.

All of the firms questioned either operate as branch offices of American-based firms or, alternatively, indicated that the United States is a country with which they conduct a significant amount of business.

Similarly, each of the respondents made reference to dealings with Far Eastern countries. On average, two out of five firms stated that they engage in business in the People's Republic of China, Japan, and Indonesia, and one firm out of five with Korea and the Philippines.

At least two of the firms questioned carry on a practice which has either an Australian or a European connection. On a lesser scale, business dealings with African countries were mentioned by one respondent, while another referred to South American business.

3.   How many lawyers are there in your office?

Each of the respondents which operates a Hong Kong branch office of a large firm employs up to six lawyers. The remaining two respondents questioned, one a Hong Kong-based firm, the other a truly international firm operating worldwide, employ thirty-three and seventy lawyers, respectively.

4.   In which area of the law does your firm practice the most?

No single area of practice is common to all of the respondents. However, there was a ninety percent response affirming practice in the following areas: banking law; debt restructuring; intellectual property law; and, international taxation. On average, two out of five firms engage in practice in the areas of antitrust law, immigration law, international finance, joint ventures and licensing agreements, litigation and transfers of technology.

The Hong Kong firms pointed to trade with the People's Republic of China as a growing area of practice.[7] Finally, conflict of laws, conveyancing, international arbitration and maritime law were each mentioned by only one firm as an area of substantial practice.

Professional Qualifications

5.   Which state bar examinations would be of the most value for a young lawyer to pass? (For example, are most of your American transactions conducted under New York or California law, etc.?)

Four out of five Hong Kong respondents favored membership in both the New York and California state bars. One of these respondents, however, a Chicago-based firm, also values the Illinois, Washington, D.C., and Arizona state bar examinations. The fifth firm, which is based in Hong Kong, stated that all of its lawyers are qualified in either Hong Kong or the United Kingdom.

6.   How important is it to your firm that your attorneys understand foreign legal systems?

Only one respondent categorized an understanding of foreign legal systems as "very important," explaining that the firm "tries to give the associates some exposure to more than one legal system." Two of the firms questioned accorded moderate importance to such an understanding. The remaining responses indicated that "a general familiarity with foreign legal systems is sufficient."

---

7. As of this writing, it is not clear as to what effect, if any, there will be on the practice of law in Hong Kong once the colony reverts to the sovereignty of the People's Republic of China in 1997.

7. Are there members of your firm who are qualified in more than one country? If yes, does this dual qualification make a job applicant to your firm significantly more attractive to your firm?

All respondents stated that some, if not most, of their lawyers are qualified in more than one jurisdiction. However, only three out of five firms described dual qualification as a significant attraction.

8. If your firm is located in England, Hong Kong, or Singapore, would qualifying as a barrister in England increase your interest in a job applicant, assuming this individual was already qualified as an American lawyer?

Only one respondent endorsed outright this additional qualification at the English bar. Two of the firms questioned, both with home offices in New York City, rejected it. The remaining two firms, while in favor of a qualification from the English bar, considered qualifying as a solicitor in England to be more valuable, since "the legal system in Hong Kong is not fused." As one respondent explained, "An ex-barrister would usually only be useful for litigation, but, for that, he must be admitted as a solicitor to work for a firm of solicitors."

9. If your firm is located in France, would earning a D.E.S.S. degree from the Université de Paris (I) increase your interest in a job applicant, assuming this individual was already qualified as an American lawyer?

Most firms had no comment in this regard. A minority of firms, however, did state that this degree would significantly increase their interest in a job candidate.

10. Do the lawyers in your office seek or accept locally-generated business?

All respondents replied in the affirmative, with just one firm stipulating that the work in question must have a non-local connection.

11. Is dual nationality an important consideration in your hiring?

There was unanimous rejection of dual nationality as a significant consideration in hiring. One international firm, however, did admit to a preference for Chinese lawyers "in view of Hong Kong's future."

12. Is it difficult to obtain a work permit for foreign lawyers in the country in which your firm is located?

None of those questioned envisioned any obstacles to securing work permits for foreign lawyers in Hong Kong.

13. Is it difficult for foreign lawyers to become members of the local bar?

All of the respondents pointed to some difficulty in this regard. Most shared the view that the level of difficulty is dependent upon the jurisdiction of a prior qualification and the duration of practice in that jurisdiction. In this respect, it seems that lawyers from the United Kingdom and other Commonwealth countries are in a more advantageous position vis-à-vis lawyers from other jurisdictions.

Educational Requirements

14. In general, would you advise a student coming out of law school, who wished to practice private international law, to qualify in a foreign jurisdiction, obtain an LL.M. in a specialty area, or go into practice with a large multinational firm?

The overwhelming response to this question favored practice with a large multinational firm, to learn what one lawyer described as the "basic skills of a lawyer."

One firm, which operates worldwide, recommended obtaining a specialty LL.M. degree or a qualification in a foreign jurisdiction in addition to practice with a large multinational firm. A Hong Kong-based firm stated that its primary requirement is that a job applicant "be qualified in Hong Kong or in the United Kingdom (by which he/she can then be admitted to Hong Kong practice)."

15. Does your firm value highly any of the following experiences for aspiring international legal practitioners? If so, why?
— LL.M. degree from an American law school in a specialty area that lends itself to international work (e.g., tax)
— LL.M. degree from a foreign university, preferably from a law school in the jurisdiction in which he/she hopes to practice in the future (e.g., EEC law, intellectual property law, international business transactions)
— M.B.A. in international business
— Clerkships
— Government experience

Ninety percent of those questioned stated that they value graduate degrees, but most emphasized that they are not a prerequisite. As one Hong Kong lawyer commented, "A postgraduate degree is not essential, but can be useful." There was considerable difference of opinion, however, as to which type of graduate degree is the most advantageous. The firms tended to be naturally biased in favor of specialty graduate work in areas in which they carry on significant practice, such as international tax, or intellectual property law. Overall, the balance between an LL.M. degree from an American law school and a foreign university was evenly divided.

Three out of five firms recommended the M.B.A. in international business. One international lawyer took the view that, "An M.B.A. can be useful since it should improve the quality of a commercial lawyer, as well as provide him with the necessary skills if he were promoted to partnership level." Another respondent considered that a business background "would be useful in a Hong Kong office in dealing with matters of China trade, foreign investment in the United States, and international finance in general."

Overall, the respondents appeared to attach less importance to clerkship experience. Some firms were uncertain as to the relevance or importance of such experience. Those who did state that they value clerkships expressed preferences for clerkship experience in areas of the law in which the firm engages in a specialized practice.

One firm approved of any China trade experience in a job applicant, and, in particular, recommended experience in the U.S. Department of Commerce (Export Administration or Licensing) for young American lawyers.

Cultural Skills

16. What qualities would your firm wish to see in the ideal candidate? That is, what kind of educational background and cultural skills should the ideal candidate possess?

The respondents appeared to look for varying qualities in a job candidate, depending upon their own specific needs. One firm expressed the view that "there is no ideal candidate; each person must be looked at *in toto*, as well as from the perspective of the specific role you wish him to fulfill." This respondent did add, however, that "a multi-racial/national background with good educational results" are primary considerations.

An American lawyer stated the basic requirement is "how good a lawyer the person is." This quality is apparently measured by "the extent of application in law school and the formative years of practice."

Two respondents saw their ideal candidate as a locally-trained individual possessing a Hong Kong or at least an English legal qualification.

Only one firm made direct reference to a background in international law as a valuable asset. This respondent went on to state that it has a particular preference for any interest, knowledge, or experience in China trade, an area in which the firm conducts significant practice.

17. How much does your firm value prior experience in a culture (e.g., time spent there during Junior Year Abroad, Summer School programs during college and law school, prior work experience, or travel)?

Three out of five firms considered prior cultural experience to be a commendable asset. For two of these firms, however, the value lies only in language skills or work experience acquired through such time spent abroad.

18. How many years of domestic practice would you recommend as a prerequisite to a young American lawyer before embarking on an international practice in a foreign jurisdiction?

The unanimous recommendation was a minimum of two years of prior domestic practice.

19. How much value do you place on language skills for applicants for an attorney position with your firm?

The majority stated that language skills are valued highly.

20. Which languages do you value most for your attorneys?

There was general agreement among the respondents that English is essential. One Hong Kong lawyer commented: "As Hong Kong is a colony of the United Kingdom, English and Chinese are official languages. All of our solicitors are conversant in English. However, all except one of our assistant solicitors recruited from the United Kingdom are not conversant in Cantonese."

The Chinese language (Mandarin, as opposed to Cantonese) is highly valued by most firms, while two out of five firms would welcome Japanese language skills. References to Indonesian, Thai, French, German and Spanish were each made by just one respondent.

JAPAN

Number of Respondents: 10

Firm Description

1. Is your office a branch office of a firm? If yes, where is the "home" office of your firm?

None of the respondents are branch offices, although one office states that it is associated with an international law firm which operates worldwide.

2. With which countries does your firm do the most significant amount of business?

A ninety percent response indicated at the outset that a significant amount of business centers around Japan itself. The United States is a country with which the majority conducts much of its business, while three out of ten firms have either Australian or European business dealings. Of interest, only two firms indicated that they conduct business with Far Eastern countries other than Japan. Overall, at least three respondents carry on a practice of a worldwide character.

3. How many lawyers are there in your office?

Seven out of ten offices questioned employ between ten and twenty lawyers. There are less than ten lawyers in the remaining three offices. The overall average is twelve lawyers per office.

4. In which areas of the law does your firm practice the most?

The responses to this question reveal that a majority of the firms questioned carry on a substantial practice in the same key areas. These areas are the following: joint ventures and licensing agreements (nine out of ten firms); international taxation (seven firms); transfers of technology (seven firms); intellectual property law (six firms); and, banking law (five firms). On average, four respondents referred to significant practice in the areas of antitrust and securities law, while three firms deal with matters of conflict of laws and corporate finance. Less than three firms engage in practice in the areas of debt restructuring, EEC law, immigration law, and mergers and acquisitions.

Professional Qualifications

5.   Which state bar examinations would be of the most value for a young lawyer to pass? (For example, are most of your transactions conducted under New York or California law, etc.?)

Half of the respondents either dismissed this question as irrelevant, or alternatively, considered it to be a helpful rather than an essential factor. Of those who expressed a preference, the overwhelming majority favored admission to the New York state bar. Some firms, however, also listed the California, District of Columbia, or Illinois state bars as valuable.

6.   How important is it to your firm that your attorneys understand foreign legal systems?

The respondents were divided in opinion in this regard. Fifty percent of those questioned declared that the issue is not significant. However, another thirty percent classified an understanding of foreign legal systems as "very important." The remaining twenty percent thought it was beneficial. As one respondent from this latter group explained: "We don't expect knowledge from law school studies, but it might make international practice more intellectually rewarding for the attorney. Most of us learn the relevant issues with respect to different jurisdictions through work experience."

7.   Are there members of your firm who are qualified in more than one country? If yes, does this dual qualification make a job applicant to your firm significantly more attractive to your firm?

Seventy percent stated that some of their lawyers possess a dual qualification. However, over half of that seventy percent did not consider this to be a significant attraction in a job candidate.

8.   If your firm is located in England, Hong Kong, or Singapore, would qualifying as a barrister in England increase your interest in a job applicant, assuming this individual was already qualified as an American lawyer?

Only one firm considered the question applicable. It stated that, "For our office, a British *solicitor* who was also an American lawyer would be very good for banking work."

9.   If your firm is located in France, would earning a D.E.S.S. degree from the Université de Paris (I) increase your interest in a job applicant, assuming this individual was already qualified as an American lawyer?

All of the respondents declined to comment.

10. Do the lawyers in your office seek or accept locally-generated business?

Sixty percent affirmed that they undertake such business. A further twenty percent stipulated that there must be a non-local connection before they will engage in locally-generated business. The remaining twenty percent had no comment.

11. Is dual nationality an important consideration in your hiring?

None of the respondents viewed it as an important consideration.

12. Is it difficult to obtain a work permit for foreign lawyers in the country where your firm is located?

The majority were of the opinion that there might be some difficulty for a foreign lawyer to obtain a work permit as an attorney, but not as a trainee. Several firms pointed to anticipated changes in the law in Japan in this regard. One lawyer explained: "...foreign lawyers will be permitted to practice in Japan as a 'foreign law attorney' from April 1987. Certain requirements must be satisfied: five years of practice in the home country, reciprocity, etc."[8]

13. Is it difficult for foreign lawyers to become members of the local bar?

The unanimous opinion is that membership in the local bar is difficult, if not impossible, for foreign lawyers. One respondent went so far as to suggest that "foreign lawyers are disadvantaged by the local bar at every opportunity." Once again, some reference was made in general to impending changes in the law.

---

8. *Special Measures Law Concerning the Handling of Legal Practice by Foreign Lawyers*, Law No. 66 of 1986 (cited as the 1986 Foreign Lawyers Practice Law). For more information, *see* John O. Hanley, "The Regulatory Regime for Foreign Lawyers in Japan," 5 *UCLA Pacific Basin L.J.* 1:1-15 (1986), and also *Practice by Foreign Lawyers in Japan*, Richard H. Wohl, Stuart M. Chemtob, and Glenn S. Fukushima, eds., American Bar Association, Chicago, 1989. (This latter publication may be ordered through the American Bar Association, Order Fulfillment, 750 North Lake Shore Drive, Chicago, Illinois, 60611, U.S.A.)

Educational Requirements

14. In general, would you advise a student coming out of law school, who wished to practice private international law, to qualify in a foreign jurisdiction, obtain an LL.M. in a specialty area, or go into practice with a large multinational firm?

Eight out of ten firms advocated going into practice with a large multinational firm. Some stipulated that such practice should involve some experience in international transactions. A minority stated that they would also be impressed by a specialized LL.M. degree. Of interest, none of the respondents recommended qualifying in a foreign jurisdiction.

15. Does your firm value any of the following experiences for aspiring international legal practitioners? If so, why?
— LL.M. from an American law school in a specialty area that lends itself to international work (e.g., tax)
— LL.M. from a foreign university, preferably from a law school in the jurisdiction in which he/she hopes to practice in the future (e.g., EEC law, intellectual property law, international business transactions)
— M.B.A. in international business
— Clerkships
— Government experience

In general, the Japanese firms did not value highly any of the options listed. Six out of ten respondents either expressed no comment or preference, or, alternatively, rejected outright both graduate degrees and clerkships. Two firms value the LL.M. from an American law school, yet none of the respondents was prepared to endorse the same degree from a foreign university. Similarly, the M.B.A. in international business was, in general, not considered to be a valuable asset in a job applicant. One Japanese lawyer did comment, however, that it is "definitely helpful in actual practice." Only two of the ten firms were enthusiastic about clerkships or government experience. One summed up the general approach in describing such experience as "not important, though not a hindrance."

Cultural Skills

16. What qualities would your firm wish to see in the ideal candidate? That is, what kind of educational background and cultural skills should the ideal candidate possess?

For half of the firms questioned, "personality" and "Japanese language skills" are the primary considerations.

Three respondents also seek a good academic background in a job applicant and, in particular, a capacity for writing was deemed to be a desirable quality.

The approach of many was summed up in one response which stated that the ideal candidate should have "...qualities required of the ideal candidate for a first-class law firm in his/her own country." "Appreciation of foreign culture," "adaptability," "English fluency," "a business background," and "work experience," are all attributes favored by only one or two firms.

17. How much does your firm value prior experience in a culture (e.g., time spent there during Junior Year Abroad, Summer School programs during college and law school, prior work experience, or travel)?

Over half of the respondents attached a high value to such experience. Some did emphasize, however, that the true value of prior cultural experience lies only in language skills or work experience gained during time abroad.

18. How many years of domestic practice would you recommend as a prerequisite to a young American lawyer before embarking on an international practice in a foreign jurisdiction?

Recommendations ranged from one year to five years of prior domestic practice, with the average suggestion being two to three years. Some reference was made to the fact that changes in the law would probably impose a minimum of five years of practice experience in the home jurisdiction prior to becoming a "foreign attorney" in Japan.

19. How much value do you place on language skills for applicants for an attorney position with your firm?

Over fifty percent of those questioned stated that they do not value language skills highly. Those who do favor such skills demand a high standard of fluency. Most respondents were of the opinion that some mastery of Japanese is useful.

20. Which languages do you value most for your attorneys?

Japanese and English were overwhelmingly endorsed by the Japanese firms as the most valuable languages. Only one out of ten respondents suggested that a European language or a mastery of Chinese might be helpful in dealing with varied clientele from China and across Europe.

PEOPLE'S REPUBLIC OF CHINA

Number of Respondents: 2

Firm Description

1. Is your office a branch office of a firm? If yes, where is the "home" office of your firm?

The respondents are both branch offices of American firms based in California. The home office of one is located in Los Angeles, and that of the other in San Francisco.

2. With which countries does your firm do the most significant amount of business?

Most of the respondents' business is conducted either with the People's Republic of China itself, or alternatively, with the United States.

3. How many lawyers are there in your office?

One office questioned maintains three lawyers, while the other employs four lawyers.

4. In which areas of the law does your firm practice the most?

Both firms referred to practice in the areas of joint ventures and licensing agreements, and transfers of technology. In addition, the Los Angeles-based firm deals with banking law, conflict of laws and international taxation, while the San Francisco-based firm practices antitrust law.

Professional Qualifications

5. Which state bar examinations would be of the most value for a young lawyer to pass? (For example, are most of your American transactions conducted under New York or California law, etc.?)

One respondent favored membership in both the New York and California state bars. The other respondent considered the California state bar to be the most valuable.

6. How important is it to your firm that your attorneys understand foreign legal systems?

Opposing views were stated in this regard. One firm stipulated that an understanding of foreign legal systems is "essential." In contrast, the other respondent concluded that "a general familiarity" with such systems is sufficient for its attorneys.

7. Are there members of your firm who are qualified in more than one country? If yes, does this dual qualification make a job applicant to your firm significantly more attractive to your firm?

Only one respondent confirmed that some of its lawyers are qualified in more than one country. However, it was not of the opinion that this dual qualification would significantly increase the firm's interest in a job applicant.

8. If your firm is located in England, Hong Kong, or Singapore, would qualifying as a barrister in England increase your interest in a job applicant, assuming this individual was already qualified as an American lawyer?

The respondents were in agreement that this additional qualification would enhance the marketability of a job candidate.

9. If your firm is located in France, would earning a D.E.S.S. degree from the Université de Paris (I) increase your interest in a job applicant, assuming this individual was already qualified as an American lawyer?

One firm replied in the affirmative, but the other respondent declined to comment.

10. Do the lawyers in your office seek or accept locally-generated business?

Both of the offices questioned engage in such business. However, the branch office of the Los Angeles-based firm emphasized that it only undertakes locally-generated business if a non-local organization is involved.

11. Is dual nationality an important consideration in your hiring?

Neither respondent viewed it as an important consideration.

12. Is it difficult to obtain a work permit for foreign lawyers in the country where your firm is located?

There was general agreement that acquiring a work permit in the People's Republic of China should not present any difficulty for a foreign lawyer.

13. Is it difficult for foreign lawyers to become members of the local bar?

The unanimous response was that it is "impossible" for a foreign lawyer to become admitted to the local bar.

Educational Requirements

14. In general, would you advise a student coming out of law school, who wished to practice private international law, to qualify in a foreign jurisdiction, obtain an LL.M. in a specialty area, or go into practice with a large multinational firm?

The respondents adopted different approaches in response to this question. The Los Angeles-based firm advocated practice with a large multinational firm. This respondent expressed the view that, "A lawyer out of law school should have some good non-international experience for at least two to four years before starting work in the international field."

The branch office of the San Francisco-based firm rejected the options listed in the question, stating that "a solid U.S. legal training and language ability should be the basics."

15. Does your firm value highly any of the following experiences for aspiring international legal practitioners? If so, why?
— LL.M. from an American law school in a specialty area that lends itself to international work (e.g., tax)
— LL.M. from a foreign university, preferably from a law school in the jurisdiction in which he/she hopes to practice in the future (e.g., EEC law, intellectual property law, international business transactions)
— M.B.A. in international business
— Clerkships
— Government experience

There was general approval of graduate degrees, although the respondents expressed divergent views as to the value of specific forms of graduate study. One firm endorsed the LL.M. from a foreign university, recommending the grounding it provides "in the language and legal attitudes of the foreign jurisdiction." This respondent ranked the other options, including clerkships, as "all a distant second."

In contrast, the second firm rejected the LL.M. degree from a foreign university, but favored the same degree from an American law school. An LL.M. degree in taxation was described as "very useful," and the M.B.A. in international business was similarly "highly regarded."

Both respondents value clerkship experience in a job applicant, although neither firm expressed a preference for a particular type of clerkship.

Cultural Skills

16. What qualities would your firm wish to see in the ideal candidate? That is, what kind of educational background and cultural skills should the ideal candidate possess?

In general, the respondents seemed to look for similar qualities in their ideal candidate. The primary stipulation was for a good domestic legal training, coupled with language skills. In addition, both firms value an ability to adapt to a foreign cultural environment, or as one respondent termed it, "a maturity to handle dealings with foreign clients."

One respondent also favored prior work experience in an aspiring international lawyer, and recommended at least two years and several summers of such experience.

17. How much does your firm value prior experience in a culture (e.g., time spent there during Junior Year Abroad, Summer School programs during college and law school, prior work experience, or travel)?

While neither firm considered prior work experience abroad to be essential, both viewed it as helpful. As one respondent commented: "We value it as an indication of international orientation, not as a direct indication of legal ability."

18. How many years of domestic practice would you recommend as a prerequisite to a young American lawyer before embarking on an international practice in a foreign jurisdiction?

A minimum of two years of domestic practice was unanimously recommended.

19. How much value do you place on language skills for applicants for an attorney position with your firm?

Language skills were valued highly in both cases.

20. Which languages do you value most for your attorneys?

The Chinese language was considered to be the most valuable. In addition, the San Francisco-based firm recommended knowledge of Japanese.

REPUBLIC OF KOREA

Number of Respondents: 2

Firm Description

1. Is your office a branch office of a firm? If yes, where is the "home" office of your firm?

Neither respondent is a branch office of a firm, although one respondent did state that it has an associate office in Los Angeles, California.

2. With which countries does your firm do the most significant amount of business?

The United States and Japan are the most significant sources of business for both firms. In addition, one respondent stated that it has dealings with a variety of countries which have business interests in the Republic of Korea, Hong Kong, the United Kingdom, and Scandinavian and Middle Eastern countries. The second firm referred to Germany as a country with which it conducts a significant amount of business.

3. How many lawyers are there in your office?

One office employs fifteen lawyers, while the other maintains a total of forty-eight lawyers (thirty-eight Korean and ten foreign lawyers).

4. In which areas of the law does your firm practice the most?

Each firm practices in the areas of intellectual property law, joint ventures and licensing agreements, and transfers of technology. In addition, one firm conducts a significant amount of business in banking law and international taxation. The other respondent pointed to insurance and shipping law as major areas of concentration.

Professional Qualifications

5. Which state bar examinations would be of the most value for a young lawyer to pass? (For example, are most of your American transactions conducted under New York or California law, etc.?)

Membership in the New York state bar is the unanimous choice, although neither firm considers it essential. One respondent commented: "While we do not require our foreign lawyers to be members of a certain bar (state or foreign), because so many transactions specify New York law as the governing law, it could be helpful for young lawyers interested in international law to pass the New York state bar examination."

6. How important is it to your firm that your attorneys understand foreign legal systems?

The responses indicate that while an understanding of foreign legal systems may be beneficial, it is by no means a prerequisite. One office which employs both Korean and foreign lawyers stated: "While we expect our foreign attorneys to have an awareness of foreign legal systems, we do not expect them to have a thorough understanding of the Korean legal system upon their arrival."

7.   Are there members of your firm who are qualified in more than one country? If yes, does this dual qualification make a job applicant to your firm significantly more attractive to your firm?

One Korean office which conducts significant practice in matters dealing with international trade stated that some of its lawyers possess a dual qualification, which the firm views as a valuable asset. In contrast, the second firm indicated that while several of its Korean attorneys are qualified in an American state jurisdiction, "we have not in the past recruited foreign attorneys qualified in more than one country, or required dual qualification."

8.   If your firm is located in England, Hong Kong, or Singapore, would qualifying as a barrister in England increase your interest in a job applicant, assuming this individual was already qualified as an American lawyer?

The respondents made no comment in this regard.

9.   If your firm is located in France, would earning a D.E.S.S. degree from the Université de Paris (I) increase your interest in a job applicant, assuming this individual was already qualified as an American lawyer?

Similarly, the respondents declined to comment.

10.   Do the lawyers in your office seek or accept locally-generated business?

The overall indication is that much of the business undertaken by the Korean firms questioned is on behalf of local clients.

11. Is dual nationality an important consideration in your hiring?

One respondent, although reluctant to describe dual nationality as "important," did conclude that it is a desirable attribute. The second firm dismissed it as a factor in the selection of job applicants.

12.   Is it difficult to obtain a work permit for foreign lawyers in the country where your firm is located?

The general view is that foreign lawyers should not encounter any difficulty in acquiring a work permit in the Republic of Korea. One lawyer suggested that admission to a bar and sponsorship by a local law firm might be prerequisites.

13.   Is it difficult for foreign lawyers to become members of the local bar?

The respondents were in agreement that the process of qualifying at the local bar is difficult, if not impossible, for foreign lawyers. One firm which employs both Korean and foreign lawyers took the view that, in the case of a foreign attorney, "while not legally impossible, it has not yet been done. In order to pass the Korean bar exam, it would be necessary to have a very thorough command of the Korean language and the Korean legal system."

Educational Requirements

14.   In general, would you advise a student coming out of law school, who wished to practice private international law, to qualify in a foreign jurisdiction, obtain an LL.M. in a specialty area, or go into practice with a large multinational firm?

Only one respondent replied to this question, offering the following insight: "In our view, the best approach is to go into practice with a large multinational law firm upon graduation from law school. Through this experience, we believe new practitioners can quickly develop a basic understanding of international law and locate those areas in which they will be able to make significant contributions."

15.   Does your firm value highly any of the following experiences for aspiring international legal practitioners? If so, why?
— LL.M. from an American law school in an area that lends itself to international work (e.g., tax)
— LL.M. from a foreign university, preferably from a law school in a jurisdiction in which he/she hopes to practice in the future (e.g., EEC law, intellectual property law, international business transactions)
— M.B.A. in international business
— Clerkships
— Government experience

Both respondents looked favorably upon graduate degrees and clerkships. A unanimous expression of preference ranked the LL.M. degree from an American law school above the same degree from a foreign university, followed by the M.B.A. degree in international business. One firm, operating a substantial practice in the fields of international trade law and intellectual property law, recommended the specialized LL.M. qualification (as opposed to a general LL.M. degree) and described it as an avenue to practice in the respective specialty area.

In the eyes of both respondents, a clerkship is a commendable achievement and valuable asset. Preferences for particular types of clerkships matched equally. Both firms conduct a specialized practice in intellectual property law and, consequently, would favor a clerkship in the U.S. Court of Appeals for the Federal Circuit (intellectual property law). Clerkship experience in the U.S. Court of International Trade (trade law) would be more valuable to both firms than a clerkship in a U.S. Tax Court (tax law), although the latter would also be an asset to a job applicant.

One firm expressed the view that while these educational experiences may prove to be invaluable, they are not a prerequisite to a job application to the firm: "Young lawyers are encouraged to work in practice for several years, and then take a leave of absence to obtain a specialty LL.M. from an American or English law school."

Cultural Skills

16. What qualities would your firm wish to see in the ideal candidate? That is, what kind of educational background and cultural skills should the ideal candidate possess?

One respondent firm expressed its view in these terms: "The ideal candidate should possess excellent academic credentials, good lawyering skills, write well, be able to communicate ideas in a clear manner, and be able to work well with other people."

The other respondent agreed that good communication skills are important. For this firm, "personality" in a job candidate is a primary consideration.

17. How much does your firm value prior experience in a culture (e.g., time spent there during Junior Year Abroad, Summer School programs during college and law school, prior work experience, or travel)?

In general, such experience is not measured with much importance by these firms. Nevertheless, most of the foreign attorneys in one of these Korean offices have spent time abroad "engaged in various endeavors during their college or law school years." Such experience, in the firm's view, has been beneficial in fostering an ability "to adjust to the demands of living overseas."

18. How many years of domestic practice would you recommend as a prerequisite to a young American lawyer before embarking on an international practice in a foreign jurisdiction?

A minimum of three years of prior domestic practice was recommended, although one firm did admit to having hired attorneys with fewer years of experience.

19. How much value do you place on language skills for applicants for an attorney position with your firm?

Fluency in the English language is a prerequisite, according to both respondents. Additional language skills, however, are not afforded a great deal of importance by either firm.

20. Which languages do you value most for your attorneys?

There was resounding agreement that in addition to fluency in English, Korean and Japanese are each of significant value.

SINGAPORE

Number of Respondents: 7

Firm Description

1. Is your office a branch office of a firm? If yes, where is the "home" office of your firm?

Four of the seven offices questioned are branch offices. Their "home" offices are located in Sydney, Australia; London, England; Chicago, Illinois; and San Francisco, California.

2. With which countries does your firm do the most significant amount of business?

Over half of the firms questioned identified the United States and Asian countries (such as Indonesia and the People's Republic of China) as substantial sources of business.

On average, two out of seven respondents referred to business with EC Member States (the United Kingdom, in particular), Hong Kong, and Japan. One firm, which is based in Singapore, pointed to business links with Australia, while another firm mentioned Kuwait.

While some of these firms have a varied international clientele and conduct business with several of the countries listed above, other respondents indicated that their business dealings are more narrowly defined. For example, one respondent operates a primarily domestic practice. Another office, with associated offices in Sydney, London, and New York, stated that the United Kingdom and the United States are its only major sources of business. Similarly, a Chicago-based firm deals exclusively with American-related matters in its Singapore branch office.

3.   How many lawyers are there in your office?

Three out of the seven offices questioned employ three lawyers. Interestingly, each of these operates as a branch office of an international multi-branch firm. The largest office, which employs thirty lawyers, stated that most of its business is locally-generated and concerns questions of domestic law. The remaining respondents employ between fifteen and twenty lawyers in their offices.

4.   In which area of the law does your firm practice the most?

Banking law is the only area of practice common to all seven respondents. However, six firms deal with joint ventures and licensing agreements, and four of the respondents conduct a substantial practice in the areas of debt restructuring, intellectual property law and transfers of technology.

A minority of firms practice in the following areas: antitrust law; building contracts; commercial litigation; conflict of laws; entertainment law; immigration law; international taxation; maritime law; and, Singapore domestic law.

Arbitration, EEC law and international finance are all areas in which only one of the respondents conducts a significant amount of business.

There are notable differences in the variety and diversification of practice among the respondents. One office, which employs eighteen lawyers, listed just three areas of substantial practice, while another office, which is staffed by three lawyers, referred to eleven separate specialties. Interestingly, both of these respondents operate as branch offices of large multinational firms.

Professional Qualifications

5.   Which state bar examinations would be of the most value for a young lawyer to pass? (For example, are most of your American transactions conducted under New York or California law, etc.?)

In general, the respondents that are branch offices of international firms tended to favor bar admissions in the jurisdiction in which the firm is based, or in which it operates another branch office. For example, a respondent firm which carries on business throughout the United States values New York or California bar memberships in potential job applicants for its Singapore office. Similarly, two international firms recommend qualifying at the English bar, and one at the Australian bar.

6. How important is it to your firm that your attorneys understand foreign legal systems?

While they did not consider it a prerequisite, most of those questioned did attach some value to such an understanding. Only one respondent dismissed it, outright, as bearing no importance. One international lawyer attached greater significance to "an outward-looking attitude." Another emphasized the quality of the legal understanding acquired, and commented that a thorough comprehension of a lawyer's own domestic legal system is more beneficial.

7. Are there members of your firm who are qualified in more than one country? If yes, does this dual qualification make a job applicant to your firm significantly more attractive to your firm?

Some lawyers in each of the respondent offices possess a dual qualification. Over half of the respondents classified it as a significant attraction.

8. If your office is located in England, Hong Kong, or Singapore, would qualifying as a barrister in England increase your interest in a job applicant, assuming this individual was already qualified as an American lawyer?

There was general agreement among most respondents that this additional qualification would increase their interest in an job candidate.

9. If your firm is located in France, would earning a D.E.S.S. degree from the Université de Paris (I) increase your interest in a job applicant, assuming this individual was already qualified as an American lawyer?

None of the respondents considered this question to be applicable to them.

10. Do the lawyers in your office seek or accept locally-generated business?

Six out of seven firms stated that they engage in locally-generated business, although one of the six stipulated that such business must have a non-local connection.

11. Is dual nationality an important consideration in your hiring?

Only one respondent considered it to be an important factor in the selection of job candidates.

12. Is it difficult to obtain a work permit for foreign lawyers in the country where your firm is located?

All of those questioned, with the exception of one international firm, remarked that there would be some difficulty in this regard.

13. Is it difficult for foreign lawyers to become members of the local bar?

The majority took the view that it is difficult, if not impossible, for a foreign lawyer to obtain a local bar qualification. One London-based firm did not agree, however, and stated that it is not difficult to be admitted, "provided a work permit can be obtained by the sponsoring firm." This respondent did suggest, though, that the process might be problematic for "non-English legal system lawyers."

Educational Requirements

14. In general, would you advise a student coming out of law school, who wished to practice private international law, to qualify in a foreign jurisdiction, obtain an LL.M. in a specialty area, or go into practice with a large multinational firm?

The respondents unanimously advocated going into practice with a large multinational firm. One Singapore-based firm stated that, ideally, an LL.M. from an English university should precede such practical experience.

An English lawyer warned of the dangers of "over-specializing." "Collecting paper qualifications is not highly regarded," he added.

One firm, practicing American and international law, offered advice of a general nature: "Some exposure to international law in any of the forms described above is useful, as it may evidence and enhance a student's awareness of cross-border cultural and legal differences."

15.   Does your firm value highly any of the following experiences for aspiring international legal practitioners? If so, why?
— LL.M. from an American law school in an area that lends itself to international work (e.g., tax)
— LL.M. from a foreign university, preferably from a law school in the jurisdiction in which he/she hopes to practice in the future (e.g., EEC law, intellectual property law, international business transactions)
— M.B.A. in international business
— Clerkships
— Government experience

All but one of the firms questioned either rejected outright, or, alternatively, was unfamiliar with clerkships. The only support for clerkships came from an American firm, which indicated that a clerkship with a U.S. Tax Court (tax law) would be valuable to their specialized practice in international taxation. Nevertheless, this respondent stated that an LL.M. degree in international taxation would be preferred.

With regard to graduate degrees generally, the vast majority recommended the LL.M. degree from a foreign university. Only two firms, both with offices and substantial clientele in the United States, favored the LL.M. degree from an American law school. An M.B.A. degree in international business was similarly endorsed by just two firms, both of which operate in a number of countries worldwide. One respondent explained that, with the experience of an M.B.A., "the understanding of the client's problems should be greater."

Cultural Skills

16.   What qualities would your firm wish to see in the ideal candidate? That is, what kind of educational background and cultural skills should the ideal candidate possess?

Over half of those questioned look primarily at academic credentials. "A good degree from a top university is assumed for all applicants," stated one international lawyer. One firm favors an emphasis on international courses in law school, while another prefers a specialized LL.M. degree. Some respondents recommended a varied educational background, and stressed the importance of an interest in another culture and the ability to adapt. For the multinational firms, a proficiency in languages is a definite advantage.

One London-based firm described an ideal candidate in these terms: "It is more a question of personality, self-motivation, application and intelligence; all must be present to an acceptable degree. A deficiency in one cannot usually be corrected by excelling in others."

17. How much does your firm value prior experience in a culture (e.g., time spent there during Junior Year Abroad, Summer School programs during college and law school, prior work experience, or travel?)

All of the respondents attached some value to prior cultural experience, although there was general agreement that it is by no means essential. One respondent warned that the significance of time spent in a culture "is not as much as might be believed by students. Certainly some travel and outside interests are expected of a candidate with the necessary self-motivation to do this kind of job, but not outside normally available vacation time."

18. How many years of domestic practice would you recommend as a prerequisite to a young American lawyer before embarking on an international practice in a foreign jurisdiction?

On average, three years of prior domestic practice is considered desirable. One firm stipulated a minimum of two years, another firm suggested a minimum of four.

19. How much value do you place on language skills for applicants for an attorney position with your firm?

While the respondents did not consider language skills to be essential, they are viewed as an asset. For most, however, only fluency in a foreign language provides any real advantage for the firm. One respondent, a lawyer with a multinational firm, suggested that language skill "is more likely to influence the possibility of a foreign office assignment, or a major client assignment, than a matter of preferring one applicant over another."

20. Which languages do you value most for your attorneys?

One firm commented that nothing is more useful than "a complete command of good English." Five out of seven respondents value Chinese (Mandarin). A minority of the firms questioned favor Japanese, Asian languages in general, and some European languages (notably French, followed by German).

SWITZERLAND

Number of Respondents: 3

Firm Description

1. Is your office a branch office of a firm? If yes, where is the "home" office of your firm located?

None of the respondents are branch offices of a firm.

2. With which countries does your firm do the most significant amount of business?

The United States and the United Kingdom were both included in each respondent's list of countries with which the most significant amount of business is conducted. For two of the firms questioned, other European countries (France and Germany, in particular) are a major source of business. The remaining respondent indicated that a substantial portion of its business has a Japanese connection. Only one respondent operates on a truly global scale, with clients from or dealings with Africa, the Middle East, Europe, and the United States.

3. How many lawyers are there in your office?

Two of the respondent offices each employ fifteen lawyers, and the third office maintains just two lawyers.

4. In which areas of the law does your firm practice the most?

Several areas of practice are common to all respondents: banking law; conflict of laws; intellectual property law; international taxation; and, joint ventures and licensing agreements. In addition, two out of three firms referred to substantial practice in litigation and transfers of technology. One of these firms, which conducts business in a variety of countries, indicated that the scope of its practice includes international arbitration, shipping finance and trade finance. The smallest of the three firms, which employs two lawyers, deals not only with international legal matters, but also with matters of Swiss domestic law, including Swiss corporate law.

Professional Qualifications

5. Which state bar examinations would be the most valuable for a young lawyer to pass? (For example, are most of your American transactions conducted under New York or California law, etc.?)

Membership in the New York state bar was recommended by all respondents. Two out of three firms also value California bar membership, while just one firm also considers Washington, D.C., and English bar qualifications to be an additional asset.

6. How important is it to your firm that your attorneys understand foreign legal systems?

One Swiss lawyer spoke for the majority: "It is considered extremely important. Most of our attorneys have also had some experience in legal studies or legal practice abroad." One respondent was less enthusiastic, and described an understanding of foreign legal systems as merely "useful."

7. Are there members of your firm who are qualified in more than one country? If yes, does this dual qualification make a job applicant to your firm significantly more attractive to your firm?

Two out of three respondents stated that some members of the firm possess a dual qualification. In the case of one such firm, it was estimated that twenty percent of its lawyers are so qualified. Both firms took the view that dual qualification is a factor which significantly enhances a candidate's employment potential.

8. If your firm is located in England, Hong Kong, or Singapore, would qualifying as a barrister in England increase your interest in a job applicant, assuming this individual was already qualified as an American lawyer?

Although all of the firms questioned carry on a significant amount of business with the United Kingdom, only one firm concluded that qualifying as an English barrister would significantly enhance the job candidacy of an American lawyer.

9. If your firm is located in France, would earning a D.E.S.S. degree from the Université de Paris (I) increase your interest in a job applicant, assuming this individual was already qualified as an American lawyer?

All the respondents stated that this question was not applicable to them.

10. Do the lawyers in your office seek or accept locally-generated business?

Lawyers in each of the offices questioned accept such business.

11. Is dual nationality an important consideration in your hiring?

For all of the Swiss firms questioned, dual nationality is an invaluable asset in a job applicant. Its importance lies in the fact that "only Swiss nationals are admitted to the bar."

12.   Is it difficult to obtain a work permit for foreign lawyers in the country where your firm is located?

There was general agreement that a foreign lawyer will encounter difficulty in acquiring a work permit in Switzerland. One respondent pointed out, however, that there are no obstacles to participating in a six-month trainee program.

13.   Is it difficult for foreign lawyers to become members of the local bar?

Without Swiss citizenship, it appears that membership in the local bar is impossible.

Educational Requirements

14.   In general, would you advise a student coming out of law school, who wished to practice private international law, to qualify in a foreign jurisdiction, obtain an LL.M. in a specialty area, or go into practice with a large multinational firm?

Two out of three respondents were strongly in favor of practice with a large multinational firm, although one of the two recommended obtaining a specialized LL.M. prior to such practice, should time permit. The remaining respondent advised any law graduate to qualify in a foreign jurisdiction. A firm which conducts a worldwide practice emphasized that the development of foreign language skills should be a priority for potential international lawyers. This respondent also recommended work experience of an international character.

15.   Does your firm value highly any of the following experiences for aspiring international legal practitioners? If so, why?
— LL.M. degree from an American law school in a specialty area that lends itself to international work (e.g., tax)
— LL.M. degree from a foreign university, preferably from a law school in the jurisdiction in which he/she hopes to practice in the future (e.g., EEC law, intellectual property law, international business transactions)
— M.B.A. in international business
— Clerkships
— Government experience

In general, graduate degrees and clerkships received some recommendation. The LL.M. degree from a foreign university was endorsed by all, the M.B.A. in international business by two out of three firms, and the LL.M. from an American law school by just one firm.

All of the respondents are impressed by clerkship experience, although some more than others. The smallest of the Swiss firms described it as "useful, but not necessary," while another firm prefers clerkships to graduate studies. With regard to individual clerkships, two out of three firms are of the opinion that federal district court and federal court of appeals clerkships are more valuable than clerkships with the U.S. Court of International Trade (trade law), the U.S. Court of Appeals for the Federal Circuit (intellectual property law), or a U.S. Tax Court (tax law), despite the fact that both firms conduct significant practice in these latter three areas.

Two firms look favorably upon government experience. One of these firms considered it superior to graduate degrees, but less valuable than a clerkship. Neither firm, however, specified the type of government experience they prefer.

Cultural Skills

16. What qualities would your firm wish to see in the ideal candidate? That is, what kind of educational background and cultural skills should the ideal candidate possess?

There was some difference of opinion among the respondents in this regard. For one firm, an excellent academic legal training and communication skills are of the utmost importance. Another respondent preferred a liberal arts background. The importance of foreign language skills was stressed by some, and all referred to "personality," or "a good manner," as essential. Finally, one Swiss lawyer concluded that a job applicant should be "well-rounded culturally," a quality which comprises "foreign exposure, language skills, and sensitivity to different cultural environments."

17. How much does your firm value prior experience in a culture (e.g., time spent there during Junior Year Abroad, Summer School programs during college and law school, prior work experience, or travel)?

The majority described such experience as "beneficial." One respondent went on to comment that "...of course, actual legal practice is ideal, but summer school programs are also well-viewed."

18. How many years of domestic practice would you recommend as a prerequisite to a young American lawyer before embarking on an international practice in a foreign jurisdiction?

The respondents did not agree on the amount of domestic work experience required for a job applicant for a position in a foreign jurisdiction. While one respondent is satisfied with one to two years of prior domestic practice, another insists on five to ten years. The third firm took the middle ground, and recommended "a minimum of two years, but, ideally, three to five." This respondent spoke of the importance of being "well-grounded as a practicing lawyer in the home legal system first."

19. How much value do you place on language skills for applicants for an attorney position with your firm?

The unanimous conclusion is that language skills are essential.

20. Which languages do you value most for your attorneys?

English and German are valued by all. Two out of three respondents recommended French language skills. One firm, which pointed to Japan as a significant source of business, welcomes knowledge of Japanese in a job applicant.

TAIWAN

Number of Respondents: 1

Firm Description

1. Is your office a branch office of a firm? If yes, where is the "home" office of your firm?

The respondent is not a branch office of a firm.

2. With which countries does your firm do the most significant amount of business?

The United States, Japan, Germany, France, the United Kingdom and Canada provide business for the firm.

3. How many lawyers are there in your office?

This Taiwan firm employs a total of five lawyers: four local lawyers, and one American lawyer who is admitted to practice in Arizona.

4. In which area of the law does your firm practice the most?

The significant areas of practice are: conflict of laws, foreign investment (inbound), intellectual property law, international trade law, joint ventures and licensing agreements, and transfers of technology.

Professional Qualifications

5. Which state bar examinations would be of the most value for a young lawyer to pass? (For example, are most of your American transactions conducted under New York or California law, etc.?)

"Generally, New York and California. However, most transnational matters require working with the lawyers *currently* practicing in the foreign jurisdiction."

6. How important is it to your firm that your attorneys understand foreign legal systems?

The respondent considers it very important.

7. Are there members of your firm who are qualified in more than one jurisdiction? If yes, does this dual qualification make a job applicant to your firm significantly more attractive to your firm?

None of the lawyers employed by the firm has a dual qualification.

8. If your firm is located in England, Hong Kong, or Singapore, would qualifying as a barrister in England increase your interest in a job applicant, assuming this individual was already qualified as an American lawyer?

Not applicable.

9. If your firm is located in France, would earning a D.E.S.S. degree from the Université de Paris (I) increase your interest in a job applicant, assuming this individual was already qualified as an American lawyer?

Not applicable.

10. Do the lawyers in your office seek or accept locally-generated business?

Lawyers in the respondent firm do seek and accept such business.

11. Is dual nationality an important consideration in your hiring?

It is not a significant factor.

12.   Is it difficult to obtain a work permit for foreign lawyers in the country where your firm is located?

In the opinion of this respondent, foreign lawyers will encounter difficulties in acquiring work permits in Taiwan.

13.   Is it difficult for foreign lawyers to become members of the local bar?

"Yes. Generally, foreign lawyers can sit for the ROC [Republic of China] bar. However, the pass rate for local candidates is usually less than one percent. To my knowledge, no foreign lawyer has ever passed the ROC bar."

Educational Requirements

14.   In general, would you advise a student coming out of law school, who wished to practice private international law, to qualify in a foreign jurisdiction, obtain an LL.M. in a specialty area, or go into practice with a large multinational firm?

The respondent stated that "any advanced training or experience in a multinational firm is potentially helpful." With regard to qualifying in a foreign jurisdiction, it was emphasized that qualifying in Taiwan is virtually impossible. As a result, "Foreign lawyers here practice under the title of foreign or international law consultant."

15.   Does your firm value highly any of the following experiences for aspiring international legal practitioners? If so, why?
— LL.M. from an American law school in an area that lends itself to international work (e.g., tax)
— LL.M. from a foreign university, preferably from a law school in the jurisdiction in which he/she hopes to practice in the future (e.g., EEC law, intellectual property law, international business transactions)
— M.B.A. in international business
— Clerkships
— Government experience

The respondent attached some value to each of the options listed, and outlined some preference for particular types of educational or training experience. Notably, no one category (graduate degrees, clerkships, or government experience) was favored over another. Emphasis was placed, however, on exposure to specialized areas in each of the three categories.

A clerkship with the U.S. Court of Appeals for the Federal Circuit (intellectual property law) was rated as the single most valuable experience. As a second preference, the respondent referred to a clerkship with the U.S. Court of International Trade (trade law), an LL.M. degree from a foreign university, or government experience [Office of the United States Trade Representative, Department of Commerce (Office of the Legal Counsel), or the International Trade Commission].

An LL.M. degree from an American law school or an M.B.A. in international business were considered less valuable than a clerkship with a U.S. Tax Court, or a federal circuit court of appeals, or government experience in the Department of State (Office of the Legal Counsel). Both graduate degrees were regarded in the same light as a clerkship with a federal district court or a state supreme court.

Cultural Skills

16. What qualities would your firm wish to see in the ideal candidate? That is, what kind of educational background and cultural skills should the ideal candidate possess?

Three factors were listed: strong research and writing ability; a background in engineering and/or business; and, two to three years of living experience in Asia.

17. How much does your firm value prior experience in a culture? (e.g., time spent there during Junior Year Abroad, Summer School programs in college and law school, prior work experience, or travel?)

Only prior work experience was considered valuable.

18. How many years of domestic practice would you recommend as a prerequisite to a young lawyer before embarking on an international practice in a foreign jurisdiction?

Two to three years of prior domestic practice was viewed as desirable.

19. How much value do you place on language skills for applicants for an attorney position with your firm?

Language skills were considered extremely important by the respondent.

20. Which languages do you value most for your attorneys?

English, Chinese, and Japanese were valued most.

THAILAND

Number of Respondents: 8

Firm Description

1. Is your office a branch office of a firm? If yes, where is the "home" office of your firm?

Two of the eight respondents operate as branch offices of large multinational firms. One such firm describes itself as "an international law firm in the true sense of the word," with no home base as such. The home office of the second firm is located in Chicago, Illinois.

2. With which countries does your firm do the most significant amount of business?

Twenty-five percent of those questioned indicated that they work exclusively within the jurisdiction of Thailand, while an additional twenty-five percent stated that work undertaken on behalf of Thai clients forms a significant part of their practice.

Most respondents listed at least three foreign countries with whom business relationships are maintained. Of these, the United States is the greatest single source of business. Of the six respondents that serve an international clientele, five stated that a substantial amount of business is conducted with the United States.

Overall, a wide variety of countries was listed, although none is common to more than twenty-five percent of the firms questioned. They include the following: Australia; European countries (France, Germany, the United Kingdom, Switzerland and the Scandinavian countries); and, Asian countries (Japan, Hong Kong, Taiwan and Nepal).

3. How many lawyers are there in your office?

Two offices employ less than ten lawyers; three offices use ten to twenty lawyers; and three offices have twenty to twenty-five lawyers each. The average is fifteen lawyers per office.

Interestingly, the smallest office among the respondents (which houses three lawyers) deals *exclusively* with domestic law and clients, while two large multinational firms responding are branch offices in Thailand, employing twenty-one and twenty-three lawyers, respectively. One Thai firm indicated that while it employs twelve lawyers in all, only one of the twelve is a foreign lawyer.

4. In which areas of the law does your firm practice the most?

The responses revealed that seventy-five percent of the firms questioned carry on a substantial practice in the areas of banking law, joint ventures and licensing agreements. Sixty percent conduct a specialized practice in intellectual property law, and forty percent deal with transfers of technology.

Other areas of concentration were identified, but in each case by less than twenty-five percent of the respondents. These areas include the following: debt restructuring; commercial financial transactions; conflict of laws; immigration law; international taxation; litigation; mineral law; and, Thai domestic law.

Professional Qualifications

5. Which state bar examinations would be of the most value for a young lawyer to pass? (For example, are most of your American transactions conducted under New York or California law, etc.?)

Most of the respondents considered this question largely irrelevant. Among those who did express a preference, admission to the New York state bar was considered the most useful, followed by admission to the California state bar. One Thai lawyer explained: "A large number of financial transactions are governed by New York law. One does not need a New York lawyer to *draft* documents governed by New York law. We use special New York counsel to review the documents as drafted."

6. How important is it to your firm that your attorneys understand foreign legal systems?

Sixty percent of those questioned attach some importance to an understanding of foreign legal systems, although none of the respondents consider it an essential requirement.

Two firms indicated that what they value most is a Thai lawyer who possesses an understanding of the British or American legal systems. Another firm suggested that attorneys should have an understanding of civil law (as opposed to common law) systems.

7. Are there members of your firm who are qualified in more than one country? If yes, does this dual qualification make a job applicant to your firm significantly more attractive to your firm?

Six out of eight firms stated that some of their lawyers possess a dual qualification. However, only half of these respondents view it as a significant consideration in the selection of job candidates.

8. If your firm is located in England, Hong Kong, or Singapore, would qualifying as a barrister in England increase your interest in a job applicant, assuming this individual was already qualified as an American lawyer?

Only twenty-five percent of the respondents stated that this additional qualification would be highly regarded.

9. If your firm is located in France, would earning a D.E.S.S. degree from the Université de Paris (I) increase your interest in a job applicant, assuming this individual was already qualified as an American lawyer?

One firm which practices in a variety of countries throughout the world considers a D.E.S.S. degree to be a significant asset for a job candidate.

10. Do the lawyers in your office seek or accept locally-generated business?

The vast majority do undertake locally-generated business.

11. Is dual nationality an important consideration in your hiring?

The respondents unanimously rejected dual nationality as a significant factor.

12. Is it difficult to obtain a work permit for foreign lawyers in the country where your firm is located?

Every firm questioned was of the opinion that it is difficult, and, in some instances, impossible to obtain a work permit as a foreign lawyer.

13. Is it difficult for foreign lawyers to become members of the local bar?

Seven out of eight respondents took the view that it is impossible. Most of those questioned made reference to the fact that the legal profession has been "a restricted occupation" since 1973, and, therefore, closed to non-nationals.

The eighth respondent took the view that qualifying at the local bar, though not impossible for foreign lawyers, is nevertheless difficult. In particular, this respondent noted that a high level of fluency in the Thai language would be essential in order to pass the bar examination.

Educational Requirements

14. In general, would you advise a student coming out of law school, who wished to practice private international law, to qualify in a foreign jurisdiction, obtain an LL.M. in a specialty area, or go into practice with a large multinational firm?

Seventy-five percent recommended practice with a large multinational firm as the most valuable option. A branch office of a large international firm which operates worldwide indicated that it would be impressed with any of the above experiences. One Thai firm which conducts a primarily domestic practice favors "practically no practice in international law." Another respondent had this to add: "Perhaps experience in a small general practice having nothing to do with international transactions is best to develop the general skills of a lawyer, i.e., common sense, etc. In seventeen years of practice abroad, I do not recall a single instance of using anything I learned in courses on international transactions in law school."

15. Does your firm value highly any of the following experiences for aspiring international legal practitioners? If so, why?
— LL.M. from an American law school in an area that lends itself to international work (e.g., tax)
— LL.M. from a foreign university, preferably from a law school in the jurisdiction in which he/she hopes to practice in the future (e.g., EEC law, intellectual property law, international business transactions)
— M.B.A. in international business
— Clerkships
— Government experience

All of the six firms that commented in this regard were in favor of graduate study experience. The LL.M. degree from an American law school was the most popular choice, followed by the same qualification from a foreign university. Three out of these six firms welcomed an M.B.A. in international business.

One respondent expressed the view that, "An LL.M. from an American or English-speaking (preferably U.K.) university insures a command of the language, as well as familiarity with our clients' way of thinking about and handling of legal problems. The specific subject studied is of little importance." One firm, which has branch offices throughout the United States, looks favorably upon an LL.M. degree, but only from an American law school, since "most of our clients are U.S. companies."

Only one respondent considered clerkship experience to be relevant, but limited its recommendation to a clerkship with the U.S. Court of International Trade (trade law). Another respondent values government experience, in particular, time spent in a legal capacity in the Department of Commerce.

Cultural Skills

16. What qualities would your firm wish to see in the ideal candidate? That is, what kind of educational background and cultural skills should the ideal candidate possess?

Half of those questioned look for solid academic achievement as a basic consideration. One respondent stated that a law degree from the United States or the United Kingdom is particularly useful. Only twenty-five percent of the respondents indicated that their ideal candidate is proficient in language skills, but forty percent considered cultural adaptability to be a significant factor.

In light of the obstacles which foreign lawyers face with regard to qualifying at the local bar in Thailand, some firms expressed a preference for Thai lawyers with international experience. As one respondent explained: "Our efforts are to employ Thai nationals holding a J.D., LL.M., or M.C.L. from institutions in the U.S."

17. How much does your firm value prior experience in a culture? (e.g., time spent there during Junior Year Abroad, Summer School programs during college and law school, prior work experience, or travel?)

The international and foreign-based firms value such experience highly, but the remaining firms dismissed it as having little or no importance.

18. How many years of domestic practice would you recommend as a prerequisite to a young American lawyer before embarking on an international practice in a foreign jurisdiction?

The average recommendation is three to five years, though many were of the opinion that it depends very much on the individual.

19. How much value do you place on language skills for applicants for an attorney position with your firm?

Half of the respondents suggested that language skills are very significant, while the other half consider them to be of moderate importance.

20. Which languages do you value most for your attorneys?

The overwhelming view is that an excellent command of English is essential. In addition, sixty percent of the respondents value Thai language skills. One multinational firm emphasized the importance of language proficiency in general, and, in particular, recommended a knowledge of Japanese, French and German. Japanese is similarly favored by one of the Thai firms.

UNITED KINGDOM

Number of Respondents: 24

Firm Description

1. Is your office a branch office of a firm? If yes, where is the "home" office of your firm?

Seventy percent of the respondents are branch offices, almost exclusively of American firms. Six firms stated that their home office is located in New York City, and three firms in Los Angeles, California. The remaining American firms are based in Atlanta, Georgia; Boston, Massachusetts; Cleveland, Ohio; Houston, Texas; Philadelphia, Pennsylvania; and Washington, D.C. The only respondent firm that is not American or English-based, has its home office in Paris, France.

2. With which countries does your firm do the most significant amount of business?

Over half of the respondents indicated that much of their business centers around the United Kingdom itself. The United States is the single greatest source of business overseas for these firms, with eleven out of twenty-four firms (both U.K. and U.S.-based) conducting significant practice with an American connection.

Most firms tend to deal with other EEC countries (France and Germany, in particular), but only a minority of respondents made reference to business dealings further afield. Five firms mentioned business with the Middle East, five with the Far East, three with Saudi Arabia, one with Canada, and one with the Caribbean.

3. How many lawyers are there in your office?

Fifty percent employ less than five lawyers in London, and the bulk of the remaining firms employ between five and ten lawyers. One English firm houses sixty lawyers in its home office in London.

4. In which areas of the law does your firm practice the most?

Joint ventures and licensing agreements is the single most popular specialty area among the respondents. Sixteen out of twenty-four firms indicated that they conduct substantial practice in that area. An average of nine firms deal with antitrust and intellectual property law, and eight firms practice banking law and structure transfers of technology.

Almost half of the respondents have a specialty practice in international taxation, and roughly one-quarter in EEC law. One fifth referred to practice in matters of conflict of laws, debt restructuring, entertainment law and immigration law. Finally, a handful of respondents deal with acquisitions, arbitration, public and private offerings, and U.K. domestic law.

Professional Qualifications

5. Which state bar examinations would be of the most value for a young lawyer to pass? (For example, are most of your American transactions conducted under New York or California law, etc.?)

One-quarter of the respondents either do not think this is important, or, alternatively, would value any bar qualification, but none in particular. There was general agreement among the respondents, however, that membership in the New York state bar is valuable. Admission to the California state bar was considered useful by some of the respondents, although, overall, it was half as popular as admission to the New York state bar. The American firms tended to favor qualifications in the state jurisdiction in which the firm is based.

6. How important is it to your firm that your attorneys understand foreign legal systems?

Half of the firms described such an understanding as "essential," or "very important," while the remainder view it as merely helpful. Three American firms dismissed it as a prerequisite to practice abroad. One such respondent considered that it is important "that attorneys assigned to London be eager to learn [but] not important that they already understand foreign law." Another commented that "... any understanding from abroad is superficial—we teach more here." Two of the larger English firms value a general understanding of legal systems in foreign lawyers, although they emphasized that greater reliance is placed on local practitioners.

7. Are there members of your firm who are qualified in more than one country? If yes, does this dual qualification make a job applicant to your firm significantly more attractive to your firm?

Lawyers in a minority of the respondent firms have a dual qualification, and few consider it to be a significant factor in hiring.

8. If your firm is located in England, Hong Kong, or Singapore, would qualifying as a barrister in England increase your interest in a job applicant, assuming this individual was already qualified as an American lawyer?

Eight respondents declared that qualifying at the English bar would significantly enhance job candidacy with their firms. Another three firms suggested that it would moderately increase their interest. Four firms (three of them English-based) stated that qualifying as a solicitor in England would be valuable, since "barristers and solicitors cannot join in partnership," and the bar "is too narrow a qualification for good office practice."[9]

9. If your firm is located in France, would earning a D.E.S.S. degree from the Université de Paris (I) increase your interest in a job applicant, assuming this individual was already qualified as an American lawyer?

Only two firms, one of which is based in France, endorsed this additional qualification.

10. Do the lawyers in your office seek or accept locally-generated business?

All of the firms questioned engage in such business. For a small number of firms, however, locally-generated business must have a non-local connection.

---

9. Since this survey was completed, a new law, the Courts and Legal Services Act of November 1990, has been adopted in the United Kingdom, allowing the Law Society to set practice rules and regulations permitting multinational partnerships (MNP's) between solicitors and foreign lawyers. To obtain a copy of this law, contact Her Majesty's Stationary Office (HMSO), 49 High Holborn, London WC2, UNITED KINGDOM. For copies of the practice rules and regulations published by the Law Society of England and Wales, in London, contact The Law Society, 113 Chancery Lane, London WC2A 1PL, UNITED KINGDOM.

11. Is dual nationality an important consideration in your hiring?

An overwhelming majority do not consider it an important factor.

12. Is it difficult to obtain a work permit for foreign lawyers in the country where your office is located?

Most respondents did not envision any difficulty in this regard. However, some suggested that the process of obtaining a work permit might prove long and tedious.

13. Is it difficult for foreign lawyers to become members of the local bar?

There was general agreement among the respondents that it could be difficult for a foreign lawyer to qualify as a barrister in England.

Educational Requirements

14. In general, would you advise a student coming out of law school, who wished to practice private international law, to qualify in a foreign jurisdiction, obtain an LL.M. in a specialty area, or go into practice with a large multinational firm?

Ninety percent of those questioned recommended practice with a large multinational firm. One respondent, a branch office of a Los Angeles-based firm, stated: "The main ingredient that makes up a good international lawyer is a good lawyer — the 'international' is something that can be learned in the field better than through a course of study, at least for international commercial practice." A New York lawyer had this to add: "The best qualification a candidate can offer is to bring work into the firm when he arrives. As compared to the U.S., unit costs are much more expensive, hence, little training time; previous experience is vital."

One American firm also recommended practice with a large multinational corporation, or, alternatively, with a government agency. An English firm suggested that practice with a small to medium-sized firm "that can offer good experience and early responsibility" is valuable.

Less than twenty percent of the firms questioned would advise a law graduate to qualify in a foreign jurisdiction or to obtain a specialized LL.M. degree. A Philadelphia lawyer, however, spoke in favor of the LL.M. degree, and against immediate practice: "If such a person could afford the time and money, an LL.M. in private international law with strong coursework could be best. Joining a multinational firm with the hope of doing international work is very chancy unless you bring real international background education or experience to the firm." One English respondent commented, regarding the type of experience chosen by law school graduates, that "it does not really matter as long as ultimately they work with a good firm in a sophisticated practice and learn basic skills from highly qualified lawyers. Obtaining an LL.M. is helpful, particularly with practical experience (preferably before the LL.M.)."

15. Does your firm value highly any of the following experiences for aspiring international legal practitioners? If so, why?
— **LL.M. from an American law school in an area that lends itself to international work (e.g., tax)**
— **LL.M. from a foreign university, preferably from a law school in the jurisdiction in which he/she hopes to practice in the future (e.g., EEC law, intellectual property law, international business transactions)**
— **M.B.A. in international business**
— **Clerkships**
— **Government experience**

Twenty-five percent of the respondents do not value highly any kind of graduate degree. In general, graduate study tended to find greater favor with the American firms. Overall, ten firms recommended the LL.M. degree from an American law school. For example, an American firm based in Los Angeles, and conducting a specialized practice in international taxation in London, would welcome a candidate with an LL.M. degree in that area. Nine firms endorsed the LL.M. degree from a foreign university, and five firms preferred an M.B.A. in international business. In general, the LL.M. degree was favored over the M.B.A. by those who expressed a preference.

None of the English firms were enthusiastic about clerkship experience, and either rejected it outright, or considered it largely irrelevant. Overall, nine firms were in favor of clerkship experience. Eight firms recommended a clerkship with the U.S. Court of International Trade (trade law), and eight with a U.S. Tax Court (tax law). Six respondents would be impressed by a clerkship with the U.S. Court of Appeals for the Federal Circuit (intellectual property law).

A small number of respondents value prior government experience, although none of these firms specified the type of government work that would be most useful. Interestingly, two firms, one French and the other American, expressed a bias against experience in government. One firm took the view that the transition from government to law firm practice "would involve a one-hundred percent change in work habits."

One Wall Street attorney remarked that, in his view, "It is most important to develop a specialty with particular relevance to international business." In contrast, another New York lawyer stated: "All the lawyers in our London office are assigned for limited periods of time on a rotational basis. Our practice does not differ significantly from our New York practice and we seek very much the same qualifications and skills." A number of responses reflected a general preference for practical experience. For example, an English barrister (who is also admitted to practice in California) commented that "substantial experience in private practice is of the only real importance."

16. What qualities would your firm wish to see in the ideal candidate? That is, what kind of educational background and cultural skills should the ideal candidate possess?

Seventeen firms emphasized the importance of a first-rate legal education, twelve the significance of language skills, and six the relevance of prior legal work experience. For many of the respondents, a combination of all three is desirable.

An ability to adapt, or, alternatively, having previous cultural experience (preferably, residency abroad) is valued by roughly one-third of the respondents. Some firms tended to emphasize qualities which they considered would be equally applicable to a candidate for a position in domestic, as opposed to overseas, practice (for example, personality, legal skills, and work habits). One American firm, which conducts a specialized practice in patents, seeks candidates with a technical background.

One respondent remarked: "The field of private international law practice is, undoubtedly, sufficiently broad that most law students with an interest should be able to find a slot that suits them. However, as a matter of plain fact, almost all of the lawyers I know in this field did not study for it, and the main credential they have is that they are skilled American business lawyers who are capable of acting as lawyers in straightforward American business matters. For this, what they need is basic legal education in hardcore topics with substantial experience in a suitable training setting."

17. **How much does your firm value prior experience in a culture? (e.g., time spent there during Junior Year Abroad, Summer School programs during college and law school, prior work experience, or travel?)**

The vast majority were prepared to attach some value to prior cultural experience, although less than half of these firms considered it to be of significant value. For most, cultural experiences are beneficial, but by no means essential. As one respondent commented, "Cultural awareness is more of a personality trait than a learned experience."

18. **How many years of domestic practice would you recommend as a prerequisite to a young American lawyer before embarking on an international practice in a foreign jurisdiction?**

There was a general consensus that two to three years should be the minimum. Six of the firms questioned, however, recommended at least five years of prior domestic practice.

19. **How much value do you place on language skills for applicants for an attorney position with your firm?**

All but one of the respondents (a branch office of a New York firm) place some value on language skills. However, less than half consider such skills to be truly significant, and one-quarter view them as a minor consideration.

20. **Which languages do you value most for your attorneys?**

The most popular foreign language among the respondents is French, which is valued by seventeen firms. Nine respondents recommended a knowledge of German. Six firms mentioned Spanish, and three respondents listed Japanese. Arabic, Chinese, Flemish (Dutch) and Italian were each favored by one or two firms.

DIRECTORY OF SUMMER AND SEMESTER INTERNATIONAL AND COMPARATIVE LAW PROGRAMS WORLDWIDE

The following is a list of international and comparative law programs worldwide, as well as available internships, traineeships and clerkships. The programs include both summer study abroad and semester degree-oriented courses open to students and practitioners. Sample course offerings are listed, where available. For more information, please contact the individual school or institution.

INTERNSHIPS, TRAINEESHIPS AND CLERKSHIPS

Canadian Summer Law Internship Program
Centre for Canadian-U.S. Law
Detroit College of Law
130 East Elizabeth Street
Detroit, MI 48201
U.S.A.
Tel. 1-313-226-0100
FAX: 1-313-965-5097

KEY ELEMENTS: Introductory courses in Canadian Law and the Canadian Legal System, followed by six-week internship placements with Canadian lawyers, judges and members of Parliament. (See entry under "Ottawa and Montreal, Canada.")

European Law Clerkships
University of Iowa
College of Law
Iowa City, IA 52242
U.S.A.
Tel. 1-319-335-9034
FAX: 1-319-335-9019

KEY ELEMENTS: Judicial clerkships in England, France, Germany and Spain. (See entry under "Arcachon, France.")

International Human Rights Internship Program
(See entry under "Fellowships" in the Advanced Degree Programs section of this *Guide*.)

International Human Rights Law Group
1601 Connecticut Avenue, N.W.
Suite 700
Washington, DC 20009
U.S.A.
Tel. 1-202-232-8500
FAX: 1-202-232-6731

KEY ELEMENTS: Summer, fall and spring unpaid legal internships. Arrangements for academic credit available.

Executive Director
International Legal Exchange Program, ABA ILEX
1700 Pennsylvania Avenue, N.W.
Suite 620
Washington, DC 20006
U.S.A.
Tel. 1-202-393-7122
FAX: 1-202-347-9015

KEY ELEMENTS: 1) Study visits overseas for groups of United
States attorneys and judges; 2) Travel and survey seminars for
groups of foreign lawyers and judges; 3) Individual placement of
United States attorneys in foreign law firms, government, or corporate law departments; 4) Individual placement of foreign lawyers
in United States firms or offices; and, 5) Coordination of programs
for United Nations or government-sponsored visitors.

The University of the Pacific
McGeorge School of Law
International Internship Program
3200 Fifth Avenue
Sacramento, CA 95817
U.S.A.
Tel. 1-916-739-7195; 1-916-739-7191 or 1-800-THE-GLOBE
FAX: 1-916-739-7111

KEY ELEMENTS: This special program, which includes six weeks
of introductory courses in Salzburg, Austria, offers numerous international law internships and clerkships worldwide. The McGeorge
School of Law also offers traineeships with barristers at its Institute
of Comparative Advocacy in London. (See entry for the Institute
under "London.")

SPECIAL NOTES

The *University of San Diego* offers a special Clinical Internship Program in conjunction with its Paris Institute on International and Comparative Law. For more information, see the University of San Diego entry under "Paris."

Other programs offering various types of internship, traineeship and clerkship opportunities include the following: *McGeorge School of Law* (London); *Pace University* (London); *University of Santa Clara* (Hong Kong); *Syracuse University* (London); and, *College of William and Mary* (Exeter and London). For more information, see the individual program listings.

Additional legal internships in international human rights law are available through the following organizations: *Amnesty International*, International Secretariat, 1 Easton Street, London, WC1X 8DJ, UNITED KINGDOM (Tel. 44-71-413-5500; FAX: 44-71-833-5100); and, *Lawyers Committee for Human Rights*, 330 Seventh Avenue, 10th Floor North, New York, NY, 10001, U.S.A. (Tel. 1-212-629-6170; FAX: 1-212-967-0916).

For additional internship opportunities in Germany, see the entry for the Young Lawyers Program of the *German Academic Exchange Service (DAAD)* under "Fellowships and Scholarships" in the Advanced Degree Programs section of this *Guide*.

For information on traineeship programs sponsored by the *International Law Students Association (ILSA)* and the *European Law Students Association (ELSA)*, contact the ILSA offices in Washington, D.C. European law students specifically interested in intra-European traineeships should contact their national ELSA organizations directly for information on ELSA's Short Term Exchange Program (STEP).

SUMMER AND SEMESTER PROGRAMS
IN INTERNATIONAL AND COMPARATIVE LAW

All programs are summer courses, unless otherwise indicated. Please note that all course offerings are subject to change. The sample course listings are for illustration only. Language of instruction is English, unless otherwise noted.

---

* = approved by the American Bar Association for credit towards the United States Juris Doctorate (J.D.) degree, as of 1990. *Check with the individual institutions or contact the Office of the Consultant on Legal Education to the American Bar Association, 55 West North Street, Indianapolis, Indiana, 46202, U.S.A. (Tel. 1-317-264-8340; FAX: 1-317-264-8355), for the latest ABA approval status.*

AFRICA

Kenya

Nairobi:

Widener University School of Law *
P.O. Box 7474
4601 Concord Pike
Wilmington, DE 19803
U.S.A.
Tel. 1-302-478-3000
FAX: 1-302-477-2282
SAMPLE COURSES: International Environmental Law, International Business Transactions, International Trade and Development Law, Public International Law

ASIA

Hong Kong, Seoul, Singapore, Taiwan, Tokyo—Internships
International Programs
McGeorge School of Law
3200 Fifth Avenue
Sacramento, CA 95817
U.S.A.
Tel. 1-916-739-7195; 1-916-739-7191 or 1-800-THE-GLOBE
FAX: 1-916-739-7111

China

Beijing:

PRC Summer Law Program-Beijing/Shanghai/Hong Kong *
American University
Washington College of Law
4400 Massachusetts Avenue, N.W.
Washington, DC 20016
U.S.A.
Tel. 1-202-885-2600
FAX: 1-202-885-3601
SAMPLE COURSES: Chinese Comparative Law, Chinese language,
International Trade Law

Director of International Programs
Loyola Law School
1441 West Olympic Boulevard
Los Angeles, CA 90015
U.S.A.
Tel. 1-213-736-1000
FAX: 1-213-380-3769
SAMPLE COURSES: Various international, comparative and for-
eign law courses in conjunction with the University of International
Business and Economics in Beijing (Tentative, beginning in 1992)

Canton:

Southwestern University
School of Law
675 South Westmoreland Avenue
Los Angeles, CA 90005
U.S.A.
Tel. 1-213-738-6700
FAX: 1-213-383-1688

Shanghai:

Foundation for American-Chinese Cultural Exchanges (FACCE)
525 West 120th Street
Box 232
New York, NY 10027
U.S.A.
Tel. 1-212-870-2525
FAX: 1-212-870-2125; 1-212-749-0397

Indiana University-Indianapolis
School of Law *
735 West New York Street
Indianapolis, IN 46202
U.S.A.
Tel. 1-317-274-8523
FAX: 1-317-274-8825
SAMPLE COURSES: Advanced Research in Comparative Law,
Constitutional Law, Criminal Law, Civil Law, Marital Law, Comparative Law (Chinese-American Law), Tax Law, Criminal Procedure, Civil Procedure, Bar System, Law of Economic Contracts, Joint Venture Law

China Program *
Willamette University
College of Law
250 Winter Street, S.E.
Salem, OR 97301
U.S.A.
Tel. 1-503-370-6380
FAX: 1-503-730-6148
SAMPLE COURSES: Chinese Law and Legal Institutions, Comparative Conflict of Laws

Hong Kong:

Summer Law Study Abroad *
Institute of International and Comparative Law
Santa Clara University
School of Law
Santa Clara, CA 95053
U.S.A.
Tel. 1-408-554-4162; 1-408-554-4361
FAX: 1-408-554-2700
SAMPLE COURSES: Trade and Commercial Relations among Hong Kong, China, and the rest of East Asia; Internships

Japan

Summer Law Study Abroad—Tokyo/Seoul *
Institute of International and Comparative Law
Santa Clara University
School of Law
Santa Clara, CA 95053
U.S.A.
Tel. 1-408-554-4162; 1-408-554-4361
FAX: 1-408-554-2700
SAMPLE COURSES: Japanese Legal System, International Business Transactions, Korean Legal System

AUSTRALASIA

ASEAN

Singapore/Bangkok/ASEAN Summer Law Study Abroad *
Institute of International and Comparative Law
Santa Clara University
School of Law
Santa Clara, CA 95053
U.S.A.
Tel. 1-408-554-4162; 1-408-554-4361
FAX: 1-408-554-2700
SAMPLE COURSES: Legal Systems and Cultures, Legal Aspects of International Investment and Development in the Countries of the ASEAN

Australia

Australian National University
Graduate International Law Program
GPO Box 4
Canberra ACT 2601
AUSTRALIA
Tel. 61.6249.0615

CANADA

Montreal:

Institute of Air and Space Law and Institute of Comparative Law
McGill University
3644 Peel Street
Room #15
Montreal, Quebec
CANADA H3A 1W9
Tel. 1-514-398-3544 (Air and Space Law); 1-514-398-1003
  (Comparative Law); 1-514-398-6666 (general university number)
FAX: 1-514-398-4655
SAMPLE COURSES: *At the Institute of Air and Space Law:* Introduction to Air and Space Law, Comparative Methodology, Economics of Air Transport, Private International Air Law I and II, Public International Air Law I, II and III, Government Regulation of Air Transport; *At the Institute of Comparative Law*: Introduction to Comparative Law, Comparative Private International Law I and II, Contemporary Private Law Problems I and II, Comparative Medical Law

Ottawa and Montreal:

Director
Canadian Summer Law Internship Program *
Centre for Canadian-U.S. Law
Detroit College of Law
130 East Elizabeth Street
Detroit, MI 48201
U.S.A.
Tel. 1-313-226-0100
FAX: 1-313-965-5097
SAMPLE COURSES: Introduction to Canadian Law and the Canadian Legal System; seminars on topical Canadian legal issues; and, speakers program. Introductory courses followed by six-week internship placements with Canadian lawyers, judges and Members of Parliament, including placements at the Department of Justice, the House of Commons, the Federal Court of Canada, major Canadian corporations and major Montreal law firms

EUROPE

Austria

Innsbruck:

Innsbruck Program *
St. Mary's University
School of Law
One Camino Santa Maria
San Antonio, TX 78284-0400
U.S.A.
Tel. 1-512-436-3424
FAX: 1-512-436-3515
SAMPLE COURSES: Comparative Law, International Business Transactions, Comparative Tort Law, Comparative Contract Law, Comparative Intellectual Property Law, Professional Responsibility

Salzburg:

Salzburg Institute on Legal Studies *
McGeorge School of Law
3200 Fifth Avenue
Sacramento, CA 95817
U.S.A.
Tel. 1-916-739-7195; 1-916-739-7191 or 1-800-THE-GLOBE
FAX: 1-916-739-7111
SAMPLE COURSES: International Business Law, Comparative Anti-Discrimination Law, Comparative Criminal Procedure, International Trade and Development Law; International Internship Program

(Alternative address:
Institute on International Legal Studies
McGeorge School of Law
Box 19
A - 5033 Salzburg
AUSTRIA
Tel. 43.662.75520
Telex: 631064.IN.LAW)

Vienna:

Vienna, Austria/Strasbourg, France Program *
Dickinson School of Law
150 South College Street
Carlisle, PA 17013
U.S.A.
Tel. 1-717-243-4611
FAX: 1-717-243-4443
SAMPLE COURSES: Comparative Law, Common and Civil Law, Trial and Appellate Practice, EEC Law, European Integration, International Transportation Law, Transnational and Comparative Criminal Litigation

Budapest/Vienna Program *
International Programs
McGeorge School of Law
3200 Fifth Avenue
Sacramento, CA 95817
U.S.A.
Tel. 1-916-739-7195; 1-916-739-7191 or 1-800-THE-GLOBE
FAX: 1-916-739-7111
SAMPLE COURSES: East/West Commerce and Law

International Relations—European Perspectives
University of Vienna
International Summer School Office
Währingerstrasse 17
A - 1090 Wien
AUSTRIA
Tel. 43.61.41; 43.61.60
SAMPLE COURSES: European Law and Institutions; International Law and the Environment
LANGUAGE(S) OF INSTRUCTION: Mostly English

Belgium

Brussels:

Brussels Seminar on the Law and Institutions of the European
    Communities
University of Georgia
School of Law
Herty Drive
Athens, GA 30602
U.S.A.
Tel. 1-404-542-5238; 1-404-542-7140
FAX: 1-404-452-5556

La Communauté européene pratique et le perfectionnement des
    langues
Université Catholique de Louvain
Centre de Langues à Louvain-la-Neuve et en Woluwe
Passage de la Vecquée 17
1200 Bruxelles
BELGIUM
Tel. 32.2.764.22.93
SAMPLE COURSES: Le Droit
LANGUAGE(S) OF INSTRUCTION: French

Brussels EEC Program (Beginning in 1992)
International Programs
McGeorge School of Law
3200 Fifth Avenue
Sacramento, CA 95817
U.S.A.
Tel. 1-916-739-7195; 1-916-739-7191 or 1-800-THE-GLOBE
FAX: 1-916-739-7111

Denmark

Copenhagen:

Duke in Denmark *
Duke University
School of Law
Science Drive and Tower View Road
Durham, NC 27706
U.S.A.
Tel. 1-919-684-2834
FAX: 1-919-684-3417
SAMPLE COURSES: Comparative Civil and Human Rights Law, Integrated Insurance Market Law, International Sales Transactions, EEC Law, Transnational Environmental Control Law

France

Aix-en-Provence:

Aix-en-Provence Academic and Cultural School
93, rue Prades
13008 Marseille
FRANCE
Tel. 33.91.53.47.81
SAMPLE COURSES: French Political Trends, European Politics, Economic Crisis

Summer Study in France *
Louisiana State University
Law Center #371
East Campus Drive
Baton Rouge, LA 70803
U.S.A.
Tel. 1-504-388-8572; 1-504-388-8491
FAX: 1-504-388-5773; 1-504-388-8202
SAMPLE COURSES: Public International Law, Comparative Law, Constitutional Law, International Commercial Arbitration, Comparative Criminal Procedure, International Human Rights Law

Arcachon:

University of Iowa *
College of Law
Iowa City, IA 52242
U.S.A.
Tel. 1-319-335-9034
FAX: 1-319-335-9019
SAMPLE COURSES: Comparative Corporate Law, Comparative Criminal Procedure, Introduction to the Law of the EEC; Participation in the program makes students eligible for the European Law Clerkships Program, which includes judicial clerkships in England, France, Germany and Spain.

Bordeaux:

Dean Rusk Center for International and Comparative Law
University of Georgia
School of Law
Herty Drive
Athens, GA 30602
U.S.A.
Tel. 1-404-542-7875; 1-404-542-7840
FAX: 1-404-542-5556
SAMPLE COURSES: Introduction to the French Civil Code, Introduction to French Commercial Law, International Business Transactions, French language immersion course

Lyon:

Minnesota-Lyon III Summer Program in European and
    International Law *
Coordinator of International Programs
University of Minnesota Law School
229 19th Avenue South
Minneapolis, MN 55455
U.S.A.
Tel. 1-612-625-4544; 1-612-625-1000
FAX: 1-612-625-3478
SAMPLE COURSES: EEC Law, Transfer of International Technology Law, International Business Transactions, International Banking Regulation, Law of Public International Organizations, Introduction to EEC Business Law, EEC Institutions and Policies

Paris:

Institute on International and Comparative Law *
University of San Diego
School of Law
Alcalá Park
San Diego, CA 92110-2492
U.S.A.
Tel. 1-619-260-4597; 1-619-260-4527
FAX: 1-619-260-4753
SAMPLE COURSES: Comparative Law, International Private Trade
Law, International Economic Dispute Resolution, Comparative La-
bor Law, International Trade and Investment Law, Public Inter-
national Law, International Business Transactions, Taxation of
International Business Transactions, International Business Law
Clinic, Survival and Intermediate French; Clinical Internship Pro-
gram

Paris Program *
Seton Hall University
School of Law
1111 Raymond Boulevard
Newark, NJ 07102
U.S.A.
Tel. 1-201-642-8500
FAX: 1-201-642-8734
SAMPLE COURSES: International Business Transactions, Inter-
national Human Rights Law, International Environmental Law

Director of Records
Tulane University *
School of Law
Joseph Merrick Jones Hall
6801 Freret Street
New Orleans, LA 70118
U.S.A.
Tel. 1-504-865-5936; 1-504-865-5939
FAX: 1-504-865-6748
SAMPLE COURSES: Two Sessions: 1) Art and the Law, Federal
Practice and Procedure, Introduction to French Law, Jurisdiction
in International Law; 2) Comparative Criminal Procedure, Consti-
tutional Law of Socialist Countries, French Civil Code as Secular
Scripture, International Aspects of Environmental Law

Strasbourg:

Summer Program Strasbourg/Geneva *
Institute of International and Comparative Law
Santa Clara University
School of Law
Santa Clara, CA 95053
U.S.A.
Tel. 1-408-554-4162; 1-408-554-4361
FAX: 1-408-554-2700
SAMPLE COURSES: Sources of International Law, International
Organizations, Human Rights Law, Comparative Socialist Consti-
tutional Law, the NIEO, Islamic Law, International Regulation of
Science and Technology

Germany

Bonn:

Western European Integration and All-European Developments
Gustav-Stresemann-Institut
Langer Grabenweg 68
D - 5300 Bonn 2
GERMANY
SAMPLE COURSES: The Legal System of the EC
LANGUAGE(S) OF INSTRUCTION: English, French, German; No
interpretation provided.

Cologne:

European and German Law
Studentenheim Schweidt
Internationale Sommerkurse
Weinsbergstrasse 74
D - 5000 Köln 30
GERMANY
Tel. 49.221.52.50.61
SAMPLE COURSES: Law of the European Communities, Legal
Questions of the Common Market, Constitutional Law of the FRG,
Introduction to the Private Law of the Federal Republic of Germany
LANGUAGE(S) OF INSTRUCTION: German, Spanish

Hamburg:

Institute of Ibero-American Studies
    im Verburd der Stiftung
Deutsches Ubersee-Institut
Alsterglacis 8
D - 2000 Hamburg 36
GERMANY
Tel. 49.40.41.20.11
A non-university center. Research is conducted on a variety of subjects concerning Latin America. The program is open to the public and private sectors, as well as academics.

Heidelberg:

Samford University *
Cumberland School of Law
800 Lake Shore Drive
Birmingham, AL 35229
U.S.A.
Tel. 1-205-870-2701
FAX: 1-205-870-2673
SAMPLE COURSES: Comparative Law

Greece

Athens:

Summer in Athens *
Temple University
School of Law
1719 North Broad Street
Philadelphia, PA 19122
U.S.A.
Tel. 1-215-787-7861
FAX: 1-215-787-1185
SAMPLE COURSES: Comparative Private Law (Greek, French, German and American), Maritime (Admiralty) Law

Thessaloniki/Rhodes/Spetsae:

Les relations Est-Ouest (Aspects juridiques, économiques,
    politiques, etc.)
Secrétariat de l'Institut de Droit International Public
Megalou Alexandrou 15 & Hadji
54640 Thessalonique
GREECE
Tel. 30.841.751; 30.810.451
SAMPLE COURSES: Les Droits de l'Homme, héritage commun ou
divisible?, La relation entre le droit international et le droit national,
Aspects économiques, juridiques des relations Est-Ouest, Problèmes
juridiques des relations Est-Ouest en Europe, Rejoignant l'Europe:
un nouvel environement politique et jurdique pour l'Europe de l'Est
LANGUAGE(S) OF INSTRUCTION: English, French (The courses
in French are simultaneously interpreted into English.)

Programs in Thessaloniki, Rhodes, and/or Spetsae *
Director of Records
Tulane University
School of Law
Joseph Merrick Jones Hall
6801 Freret Street
New Orleans, LA 70118
U.S.A.
Tel. 1-504-865-5936; 1-504-865-5939
FAX: 1-504-865-6748
SAMPLE COURSES: *Classes in Spetsae:* Law of Freedom of Speech,
International Organizations Law, European Communities Law, Pri-
vate International Law; *Classes in Rhodes:* Maritime Torts Law (Per-
sonal Injury, Wrongful Death), International Civil Litigation, Private
International Law, International Carriage of Goods, Comparative
Federalism

Hungary

Budapest:

International Programs Budapest/Vienna *
McGeorge School of Law
3200 Fifth Avenue
Sacramento, CA 95817
U.S.A.
Tel. 1-916-739-7195; 1-916-739-7191 or 1-800-THE-GLOBE
FAX: 1-916-739-7111
SAMPLE COURSES: East/West Commerce and Law

Cardozo in Budapest Summer Program *
Office of Admissions
Benjamin N. Cardozo School of Law
Yeshiva University
55 Fifth Avenue
New York, NY 10003
U.S.A.
Tel. 1-212-790-0274, 1-212-790-0200
FAX: 1-212-790-0345
SAMPLE COURSES: Emerging Constitutionalism in Eastern Europe: A Comparative Perspective; Freedom, Communications Policy and New Technology; Issues in International Trade Transactions

Ireland

Dublin:

Institute on International and Comparative Law *
University of San Diego
School of Law
Alcalá Park
San Diego, CA 92110-2492
U.S.A.
Tel. 1-619-260-4597; 1-619-260-4527
FAX: 1-619-260-4753
SAMPLE COURSES: International Trade and Investment Law, International Human Rights Law, Comparative Civil Rights Law, Comparative Criminal Justice, Irish Legal System

Summer Law in Ireland *
University of San Francisco
School of Law
2130 Fulton
San Francisco, CA 94117-1080
U.S.A.
Tel. 1-415-666-6307
FAX: 1-415-666-6433
SAMPLE COURSES: Comparative Law, the English and Irish Legal Systems, Comparative Civil Liberties Law, EEC Law, Evidence, Public International Law

Italy

Aosta:

La théorie du federalisme global
Centre International de Formation Européenne
Direction générale
4, Boulevard Carabacel
06000 Nice
FRANCE
Tel. 33.93.85.85.57
SAMPLE COURSES: Aspects juridico-politiques
LANGUAGE(S) OF INSTRUCTION: French

Florence:

Le Droit Communautaire et la Protection des Droits de l'Homme
Académie de Droit Européen
C.P. no. 2330
50100 Firenze Ferrovia
ITALY
Tel. 39.55.5092256; 39.55.576195
FAX: 39.55.587197
SAMPLE COURSES: Droit communautaire; Protection des Droits
de l'Homme
LANGUAGE(S) OF INSTRUCTION: English or French (with si-
multaneous translation into the other language)

Summer Seminar in Florence *
Dickinson School of Law
150 South College Street
Carlisle, PA 17013
U.S.A.
Tel. 1-717-243-4611
FAX: 1-717-243-4443
SAMPLE COURSES: Comparative Law, Common and Civil Law
Trial and Appellate Practice, EEC Law, Comparative Civil and
Criminal Procedure, Transnational and Comparative Criminal Lit-
igation

Summer Law Program in Florence *
Georgetown University Law Center
600 New Jersey Avenue, N.W.
Washington, DC 20001
U.S.A.
Tel. 1-202-662-9320; 1-202-662-9000; or 1-800-346-6259
FAX: 1-202-662-9444
SAMPLE COURSES: Public International Law I and II, International Business and Economic Law, Constitutional Law II, EEC Law, and Comparative Business Law Seminar

Padua:

Padua Summer Law Institute *
Widener University
School of Law
Admissions Office
P.O. Box 7474
4601 Concord Pike
Wilmington, DE 19803
U.S.A.
Tel. 1-302-478-3000
FAX: 1-302-477-2282
SAMPLE COURSES: Introduction to Civil Law, EEC Law, International Business Transactions, Comparative Health Law, Dispute Resolution in a Comparative Setting

Parma:

Seton Hall University *
School of Law
1111 Raymond Boulevard
Newark, NJ 07102
U.S.A.
Tel. 1-201-642-8500
FAX: 1-201-642-8734
SAMPLE COURSES: Comparative Torts, History of the Western Legal Tradition, International Business Transactions

Rome:

Loyola University of Chicago *
School of Law
1 East Pearson Street
Chicago, IL 60611
U.S.A.
Tel. 1-312-915-7120
FAX: 1-312-337-5797
SAMPLE COURSES: Comparative Constitutional Law (Europe, United States and Third World countries), Estates, International Business Transactions, Roman Law

International Program — Rome *
Temple University School of Law
1719 North Broad Street
Philadelphia, PA 19122
U.S.A.
Tel. 1-215-787-7861
FAX: 1-215-787-1185
SAMPLE COURSES: Common Law and Civil Law Traditions, Comparative Constitutional Law, Introduction to Common Market Law and Institutions

Siena:

Director of Records
Tulane University *
School of Law
Joseph Merrick Jones Hall
6801 Freret Street
New Orleans, LA 70118
U.S.A.
Tel. 1-504-865-5936; 1-504-865-5939
FAX: 1-504-865-6748
SAMPLE COURSES: Comparative Constitutional Law, Comparative Law (United States and the EEC) and Policies Relating to International Trade, EEC Law, History and Anthropology of Law, International Banking Law, Products Liability Law, International Law and the Use of Coercion, Continuing legal education seminar on International Environmental Law and Antarctica

Urbino:

Séminaire de Droit Européen d'Urbino
235, Boulevard Saint-Denis
92400 Courbevoie
FRANCE
Tel. 33.43.33.73.05
SAMPLE COURSES: Le rôle de la volonté individuelle dans les codifications récentes de droit international privé, Terminologie juridique franco-italienne, Le nouveau droit italien de la famille dans la jurisprudence, Le droit européen des sociétés anonymes, Le contrat de travail en droit international privé, Le droit de la personne et de la famille dans le projet de la réforme du droit international italien, La théorie de l'acte unique dans le droit communautaire
LANGUAGE(S) OF INSTRUCTION: French or Italian (with a summary translation into the other language)

The Netherlands

Amsterdam:

Amsterdam-Leiden-Columbia
Summer Program in American Law
University of Amsterdam
Oudezijds Achterburgwal 217
1012 DL Amsterdam
THE NETHERLANDS
Tel. 31.20.52.53.439
SAMPLE COURSES: Legal Methods, Civil Procedure, Constitutional Law, optional courses; (Introduction to American Law for European-trained lawyers. Instruction is based on American methods and includes discussions based on prior study. Cooperating organizations are Leiden University and Columbia University.)

Legal Aspects of European Integration
The Amsterdam School for Executive Development in
    International Relations (ASEDIR)
University of Amsterdam
Oudezijds Achterburgwal 237
1012 DL Amsterdam
THE NETHERLANDS
Tel. 31.20.52.52.966
FAX: 31.20.52.52.086
SAMPLE COURSES: Judicial Remedies, Substantive Law of the European Communities, Antitrust/Competition Law, Intellectual Property Law, Company Law and Free Circulation of Goods

The Hague:

The Hague Academy of International Law
Peace Palace
Carnegieplein 2
2517 KJ The Hague
THE NETHERLANDS
Tel. 31.70.46.96.80
SAMPLE COURSES: *Two Sessions*: 1) Private International Law
courses; 2) Public International Law courses

Leiden:

International Summer Course
State University of Leiden
Faculty of Law
P.O. Box 9500
2300 RA Leiden
THE NETHERLANDS
Tel. 31.71.27.76.28.
FAX: 31.71.27.76.00
SAMPLE COURSES: Law of the European Communities, Law in
the Soviet Union and Perestroika, European Products Liability,
General Principles of International Private Law

Norway

Oslo:

University of North Dakota *
School of Law
Grand Forks, ND 58202
U.S.A.
Tel. 1-701-777-2691
FAX: 1-701-777-2217
SAMPLE COURSES: Comparative Law, International Law, Human
Rights Law

Poland

Program in Russia/Poland *
Institute on International and Comparative Law
University of San Diego
School of Law
Alcalá Park
San Diego, CA 92110-2492
U.S.A.
Tel. 1-619-260-4597; 1-619-260-4527
FAX: 1-619-260-4753
SAMPLE COURSES: East/West Trade Law, Socialist Law

Spain

Barcelona:

Spanish-German Legal Courses
Studentenheim Schweidt
Internationale Sommerkurse
Weinbergstrasse 74
D - 5000 Köln 30
GERMANY
Tel. 49.221.52.50.61
SAMPLE COURSES: The Adaptation of Spanish Law to Community
Law, Spanish Constitutional Law, Specific Aspects of Spanish
Private Law
LANGUAGE(S) OF INSTRUCTION: German, Spanish

Madrid:

Summer School of Law in Europe *
College of William and Mary
Marshall-Wythe School of Law
South Henry Street
Williamsburg, VA 23185
U.S.A.
Tel. 1-804-221-3818; 1-804-221-3800
FAX: 1-804-221-3261
SAMPLE COURSES: Spanish Constitutional Law and Policy, In-
troduction to Civil Law, European Civil Rights Law, The EEC Le-
gal System, Comparative Administrative Law

Toledo:

Summer Program in Spain *
Catholic University of Puerto Rico
School of Law
Ponce, PR 00732
U.S.A.
Tel. 1-809-841-2000, ext. 341 or 342 (Ponce);
    1-809-793-3720 (San Juan)
FAX: 1-809-841-4620 (Ponce);
    1-809-793-3720 (San Juan)
SAMPLE COURSES: New Trends in the Civil Law System, His-
torical and Judicial Aspects of Spain's Constitutional Transition, The
Constitutionalization of Spain's Civil Law, The Economic Model of
Spain's Constitution, Historical and Contemporary Problems of the
Process of Codification of Civil Law, New Trends in Property Law,
Contracts and Family Law, The Autonomous Regimes and Their
Impact on the Development of Civil Law in Spain. Conferences are
also offered at the University of Salamanca School of Law and the
University of Barcelona School of Law.
LANGUAGES OF INSTRUCTION: Spanish

Sweden

Lund:

Institute of International Law
Lund University
P O Box 1165 S-221 05 Lund
SWEDEN
Tel. 46.46.10.80.74
FAX: 46.46.10.44.45
THREE COURSES: 1) Public International Law (5 weeks);
2) Human Rights and Humanitarian Law (5 or 10 weeks); and,
3) Public International Law: Advanced Courses in Human Rights
and Humanitarian Law (18 weeks)

Stockholm:

Assistant to the Dean of International Studies
Faculty of Law
Stockholm University
S-106 91 Stockholm
SWEDEN
Tel. 46.8.16.26.14
FAX: 46.8.15.95.22
SPECIAL COURSE: Legal English (English for the Legal
Profession)

Uppsala:

Minnesota-Uppsala University Summer Program in International
    and Comparative Legal Studies *
Coordinator of International Programs
University of Minnesota Law School
229 19th Avenue South
Minneapolis, MN 55455
U.S.A.
Tel. 1-612-625-4544; 1-612-625-1000
FAX: 1-612-625-3478
SAMPLE COURSES: Introduction to European Law, Access to
Justice, Comparative Biomedical Ethics, Comparative Antitrust Law,
EEC Law, Introduction to Scandinavian Law, Environmental Law—
International and American Perspectives, Legal Aspects of Invest-
ment in the Soviet Union, Peace and Security in Northern Europe
(held in Leningrad, U.S.S.R.)

Switzerland

Fribourg:

Territorial distribution of power in Europe
Institute of Federalism
University Misericorde
CH - 1700 Fribourg
SWITZERLAND
Tel. 41.37.219.591
FAX: 41.37.219.701
SAMPLE COURSES: Introductory Course on the Law of Decen-
tralization and Self-government
LANGUAGE(S) OF INSTRUCTION: English, French

Geneva:

Strasbourg/Geneva Program *
Institute of International and Comparative Law
Santa Clara University
School of Law
Santa Clara, CA 95053
U.S.A.
Tel. 1-408-554-4162; 1-408-554-4361
FAX: 1-408-554-2700
SAMPLE COURSES: Sources of International Law, Law of International Organizations, Human Rights Law, Comparative Socialist Constitutional Law, the NIEO, Islamic Law, International Regulation of Science and Technology

U.S.S.R.

Russia/Poland Program *
Institute on International and Comparative Law
University of San Diego
School of Law
Alcalá Park
San Diego, CA 92110-2492
U.S.A.
Tel. 1-619-260-4597; 1-619-260-4527
FAX: 1-619-260-4753
SAMPLE COURSES: East/West Trade Law, Socialist Law
(See also entry for "Uppsala.")

United Kingdom (*England*)

Cambridge:

Cambridge Summer Session *
University of Mississippi
School of Law
University, MS 38677
U.S.A.
Tel. 1-601-232-7361
FAX: 1-601-232-7731
SAMPLE COURSES: Comparative Social Legislation, Public International Law, International Trade Law, Common Market Law, Comparative Law, English Legal History

Summer Program in Law at Cambridge *
University of Richmond
The T.C. Williams School of Law
Richmond, VA 23173
U.S.A.
Tel. 1-804-289-8740
FAX: 1-804-289-8683
SAMPLE COURSES: International Law, Legal History, Comparative Public Law of the United States and the United Kingdom, EEC Law, Wills and Trusts, Administrative Law

Director of Records
Tulane University *
School of Law
Joseph Merrick Jones Hall
6801 Freret Street
New Orleans, LA 70118
U.S.A.
Tel. 1-504-865-5936; 1-504-865-5939
FAX: 1-504-865-6748
SAMPLE COURSES: Historical Aspects of the English Legal System, Foreign Trade Policy and Taxation, EEC Law, Comparative Family Law; (two sessions—courses may differ)

Canterbury:

Samford University *
Cumberland School of Law
800 Lake Shore Drive
Birmingham, AL 35229
U.S.A.
Tel. 1-205-870-2701
FAX: 1-205-870-2673
SAMPLE COURSES: International Business Transactions, EEC Law, English Legal System, Comparative Corporate Law

Exeter:

Courses in European Community Law
Secretary, CELS
Law Faculty, University of Exeter
Amory Building, Rennes Drive
Exeter EX4 4RJ
UNITED KINGDOM
Tel. 44-392-26-3380
SAMPLE COURSES: The Practical Scope of EEC Law, Competition Law, Intellectual Property under EC Law, The European Court of Justice, Use of Computerized Legal Databases in EC Law, Protection of the Environment under EC Law, Sex Discrimination and EC Law, Contracts: Choice of Law Problems, Recent Developments in Community Company Law.

Exeter (and London):

Summer School of Law in England *
College of William and Mary
Marshall-Wythe School of Law
South Henry Street
Williamsburg, VA 23185
U.S.A.
Tel. 1-804-221-3818; 1-804-221-3800
FAX: 1-804-221-3261
SAMPLE COURSES: International Law, International Business Transactions, Insurance Law, Mass Media Law, Civil Rights Law, Labor Law, Federal Courts and the Federal System, Employment Discrimination Law, Introduction to Civil Law; Legal Clerking

London:

Program at Kings College * (fall or spring semester; varies from year-to-year)
Boston College Law School
885 Centre Street
Newton, MA 02159
U.S.A.
Tel. 1-617-552-8550
FAX: 1-617-552-2615
SAMPLE COURSES: International Law, Comparative Law, EEC Law

London Law Programme * (fall or spring semester available)
University of Detroit
School of Law
651 East Jefferson Avenue
Detroit, MI 48226
U.S.A.
Tel. 1-313-596-0200
FAX: 1-313-596-0280
SAMPLE COURSES: International Business Transactions, International Commercial Arbitration, International Air and Space Law, Common Market Law

Summer Courses in European Community Law
Centre of European Law
King's College
Strand
London WC2R 2LS
UNITED KINGDOM
Tel. 44-71-240-0206
SAMPLE COURSES: Introduction to the Community Legal System, EEC Company Laws, EEC Competition Law, The European Court of Justice and Judicial Remedies, Jurisdiction and Enforcement of Judgments in the EEC

International Program-London *
Institute of International Business and Commerical Law
McGeorge School of Law
3200 Fifth Avenue
Sacramento, CA 95817
U.S.A.
Tel. 1-916-739-7195; 1-916-739-7191 or 1-800-THE-GLOBE
FAX: 1-916-739-7111
SAMPLE COURSES: International Business Transactions, Fundamental Rights Law in Europe and the United States, Trade Law with Japan, Law of International Sale of Goods; Internships (Beginning in 1991, further emphasis will be placed on EEC law.)

International Program—London *
Institute of Comparative Advocacy
McGeorge School of Law
3200 Fifth Avenue
Sacramento, CA 95817
U.S.A.
Tel. 1-916-739-7195; 1-916-739-7191 or 1-800-THE-GLOBE
FAX: 1-916-739-7111
SAMPLE COURSES: The London Institute of Comparative Advocacy provides an advocacy course consisting of lectures and training in chambers with barristers in commerical, penal and family law.

London Law Programme * (also full-year program available)
Notre Dame Law School
Notre Dame, IN 46556
U.S.A.
Tel. 1-219-239-6627
FAX: 1-219-239-6371
SAMPLE COURSES: Common Market Law, English Legal System, Jurisprudence, Public International Law, International Human Rights Law, Evidence, Art Law, International Business Law, Introduction to the Soviet Legal System, Comparative Law

Pace London Law Program * (spring semester)
Pace University
School of Law
78 North Broadway
White Plains, NY 10603
U.S.A.
Tel. 1-914-422-4252; 1-914-422-4205
FAX: 1-914-422-4139
SAMPLE COURSES: International Trade Law, EEC Law, British Legal System, Conflict of Laws—Interstate and International, Evidence, Corporations, Remedies; Internships

London Program * (fall semester)
Pepperdine University
School of Law
24255 Pacific Coast Highway
Malibu, CA 90265-9989
U.S.A.
Tel. 1-213-456-4611
FAX: 1-213-456-4266
SAMPLE COURSES: Evidence, Commercial Law—Secured Transactions and Commercial Paper, Corporations, Common Law, Contemporary European Trade, International Public Law, Law of the Sea, Comparative Legal Process; (Pepperdine students receive preference.)

Commercial Law Summer School
Centre for Commercial Law Studies
Queen Mary College
339 Mile End Road
London E1 4NS
UNITED KINGDOM
Tel. 44-71-975-5127; 44-71-975-5555
FAX: 44-71-980-1079
SAMPLE COURSES: A program of advanced one-week courses in: National and International Licensing of Intellectual Property, Contemporary Problems in International Sales Law, Securities Regulation, Commercial Arbitration, Drafting International Finance Documents

Summer Law Program London *
Institute on International and Comparative Law
University of San Diego
School of Law
Alcalá Park
San Diego, CA 92110-2492
U.S.A.
Tel. 1-619-260-4597; 1-619-260-4527
FAX: 1-619-260-4753
SAMPLE COURSES: International Litigation, Comparative Law, International Finance Law, International Contracts and Negotiations, International Trade Law, International Corporate Law, International Business Transactions, International Commercial Arbitration; Clinical Internships

Summer Law Program in London *
Division of International Programs
Syracuse University
College of Law
119 Euclid Avenue
Syracuse, NY 13244
U.S.A.
Tel. 1-315-443-2524
FAX: 1-315-453-9568
SAMPLE COURSES: English Legal System; Clinical Internship
Program

Intensive Foundation—EEC Law and Practice
University College London
Faculty of Laws
UCLI Limited
5 Gower Street
London WC1E 6HA
UNITED KINGDOM
Tel. 44-71-636-7668
FAX: 44-71-637-7921
SAMPLE COURSES: Competition Law, Intellectual Property Law,
Trade Law, Corporate Structure and Company Law in the Single
Market

London Summer Program *
Wake Forest University
School of Law
P.O. Box 7206
Carswell Hall
Wingate Drive
Winston-Salem, NC 27109
U.S.A.
Tel. 1-919-759-5435; 1-919-759-5430
FAX: 1-919-759-6077

Anglo-American Comparative Law Program *
William Mitchell College of Law
875 Summit Avenue
St. Paul, MN 55105
U.S.A.
Tel. 1-612-227-9171
FAX: 1-612-290-6414
SAMPLE COURSES: Comparative Judicial Administration, Comparative Constitutional Jurisprudence, Independent Research in Comparative Law Topics

LONDON CONSORTIUM: University of Arizona, Arizona State University, Indiana University—Bloomington, University of Iowa, University of Kansas, University of Utah; (For further information, contact the individual schools.)

Oxford:

Summer Program in Law at Oxford *
Florida State University
College of Law
Box F
Tallahassee, FL 32306-1034
U.S.A.
Tel. 1-904-644-4578; 1-904-644-3400
FAX: 1-904-644-5216; 1-904-644-5487
SAMPLE COURSES: English Legal History, EEC Law, Comparative Law, American law courses

Ohio State University *
College of Law
1659 North High Street
Columbus, OH 43210
U.S.A.
Tel. 1-614-292-2631
FAX: 1-614-292-3202
SAMPLE COURSES: Comparative Criminal Justice, International Trade Law, Licensing and Investment Law, Comparative Legal Professions

Summer Program at Oxford *
University of Oklahoma
Law Center
300 Timberdell Road
Norman, OK 73019
U.S.A.
Tel. 1-405-325-4699
FAX: 1-405-325-6282
SAMPLE COURSES: Professional Responsibility, International Business Transactions, Energy and Natural Resources Law, British Constitutional Law and Institutions, English Legal Process, EEC Law

Oxford Study Abroad Summer Program *
Institute on International and Comparative Law
University of San Diego
School of Law
Alcalá Park
San Diego, CA 92110-2492
U.S.A.
Tel. 1-619-260-4597; 1-619-260-4527
FAX: 1-619-260-4753
SAMPLE COURSES: Public International Law, EEC Law, Unjust Enrichment, Medical-Legal Problems, Civil Liberties Law, Comparative Criminal Justice

Oxford Summer Program *
Summer Law Study Abroad
Santa Clara University
School of Law
Santa Clara, CA 95053
U.S.A.
Tel. 1-408-554-4162; 1-408-554-4361
FAX: 1-408-554-2700
SAMPLE COURSES: Civil Liberties Law (selected problems), Jurisprudence, English Legal History, EEC Law

Oxford Summer Program *
Southern Methodist University
School of Law
Dallas, TX 75275
U.S.A.
Tel. 1-214-692-2618
FAX: 1-214-692-4330
SAMPLE COURSES: Sales of Goods, International Trade Law,
Public International Law, Evidence

Uxbridge (and London):

Washburn University *
School of Law
1700 College
Topeka, KS 66621
U.S.A.
Tel. 1-913-295-6660
FAX: 1-913-232-8087
SAMPLE COURSES: Comparative Legal Systems, Comparative
Consumer Credit and Protection Law, Comparative Regulation of
Rural and Public Land, Comparative Criminal Justice Administra-
tion, Comparative Issues in Transfers of Wealth

United Kingdom (*Scotland*)

Aberdeen:

Foreign Law Program — Aberdeen *
University of Baltimore
School of Law
1420 North Charles Street
Baltimore, MD 21201
U.S.A.
Tel. 1-301-625-3170
FAX: 1-301-625-3207
SAMPLE COURSES: Comparative Criminal Justice, Professional
Responsibility, Comparative Legal Profession

Edinburgh:

Edinburgh Summer Program *
Southern Methodist University
School of Law
Dallas, TX 75275
U.S.A.
Tel. 1-214-692-2618
FAX: 1-214-692-4330
SAMPLE COURSES: Legal Problems of International Business, Comparative Law, International Law

Glasgow:

European Law Programme
School of Law
University of Glasgow
Glasgow G12 8QQ
UNITED KINGDOM
Tel. 44-41-339-8855
FAX: 44-41-330-4900
SAMPLE COURSES: European Legal Systems, Law of the Economy in the EEC, Commercial Law in the United Kingdom, Human Rights

LATIN AMERICA/CARIBBEAN

Argentina

Buenos Aires:

Coordinator
Sección de Derecho Internacional
Centro de Estudios Internacionales de Buenos Aires
San Martin 522 - Piso 4to - Oficinas 9 y 10
Capital Federal 1004 (Buenos Aires)
ARGENTINA
Tel. 54-1-393-1196
FAX: 54-1-393-1196
SAMPLE COURSES: Research projects, publications, and postgraduate seminars in International Law, Human Rights, and Economic Intergration (2-3 month summer courses)

Brazil

Brasilia:

Instituto de Rio Branco
Universidade de Brasilia
Agencia Postale 15
70910 Brasilia, DF
BRAZIL
SAMPLE COURSES: International Law and International
Relations

Chile

Santiago, Valparaiso and Farellones:

Chile Summer Law Program *
American University
Washington College of Law
4400 Massachusetts Avenue, N.W.
Washington, DC 20016
U.S.A.
Tel. 1-202-885-2600
FAX: 1-202-885-3601
SAMPLE COURSES: Introduction to International Trade with Latin
America, Comparative Law, The Civil Law Tradition

Costa Rica

San Juan:

Director of International Programs *
Loyola Law School
1441 West Olympic Boulevard
Los Angeles, CA 90015
U.S.A.
Tel. 1-213-736-1000
FAX: 1-213-380-3769
SAMPLE COURSES: Various international, comparative and for-
eign law courses, with some sessions held in Managua, Nicaragua

Cuba

Havana:

University of Havana
c/o Inter-American Comparative Law Institute
65-21 Main Street
Flushing, NY 11367
U.S.A.
Tel. 1-718-575-4318; 1-718-575-4200
FAX: 1-718-575-4275

Guatemala

Campbell University *
Norman Adrian Wiggins School of Law
P.O. Box 158
Buies Creek, NC 27506
U.S.A.
Tel. 1-919-893-2773
FAX: 1-919-893-9850
SAMPLE COURSES: Immigration and Refugee Law, Private International Law, Seminar on Legal Issues in Developing Nations

Mexico

Cuernavaca:

Loyola University of New Orleans *
7214 St. Charles Avenue
New Orleans, LA 70118
U.S.A.
Tel. 1-504-861-5550
FAX: 1-504-861-5895
SAMPLE COURSES: Comparative Law, United States Immigration and Naturalization Law

Guanajuato:

Summer Law Institute of the
    University of New Mexico
    School of Law
University of New Mexico
Latin American Institute
801 Yale N.E.
Albuquerque, NM 87131
U.S.A.
Tel. 1-505-277-2961
FAX: 1-505-277-5989
SAMPLE COURSES: Six-week and eight-week programs in international business law and comparative civil and criminal law practice; (Programs organized jointly with the University of New Mexico School of Law, the Latin American Institute, and the Facultad de Derecho of the University of Guanajuato.)

Mexico City:

Mexican Legal Studies Program *
University of Houston
Law Center
4800 Calhoun Road
Houston, TX 77004-6370
U.S.A.
Tel. 1-713-749-7263; 1-713-749-1422
FAX: 1-713-749-2567
SAMPLE COURSES: Mexican Law I—Introduction to the Mexican Legal System, Mexican Law II—Legal Aspects of Foreign Investment in Mexico, United States-Mexican Conflict of Laws, Immigration Law and Policy, International Banking Law

Mexican Summer Law Program
Notre Dame Law School
Notre Dame, IN 46556
U.S.A.
Tel. 1-219-239-6627
FAX: 1-219-239-6371
SAMPLE COURSES: Comparative Law, International Business Transactions, International Law and Human Rights, Economic Policy and the Law—Development in the Western Hemisphere

Mexico Program *
Institute on International and Comparative Law
University of San Diego
School of Law
Alcalá Park
San Diego, CA 92110-2492
U.S.A.
Tel. 1-619-269-4597; 1-619-260-4527
FAX: 1-619-260-4753
SAMPLE COURSES: Immigration Law, Public International Law,
International Business Transactions, Mexican Trade and Invest-
ment Law, Survival Spanish, Legal Spanish

Nicaragua

Managua:

Director of International Programs *
Loyola Law School
1441 West Olympic Boulevard
Los Angeles, CA 90015
U.S.A.
Tel. 1-213-736-1000
FAX: 1-213-380-3769
SAMPLE COURSES: Various international, comparative and for-
eign law courses, with main sessions held in San Juan, Costa Rica.

West Indies (*Barbados*)

Florida State University *
College of Law
425 W. Jefferson Street
Tallahassee, FL 32306-1034
U.S.A.
Tel. 1-904-644-7297; 1-904-644-3400
FAX: 1-904-644-5487
SAMPLE COURSES: Civil Liberties in the Commonwealth
Caribbean, Foreign Investment Law in the Commonwealth
Caribbean, Current Problems in Immigration Law, Legal Institutions
of the Commonwealth Caribbean

MIDDLE EAST

Israel

Jerusalem:

Director of Records
Tulane University *
School of Law
Joseph Merrick Jones Hall
6801 Freret Street
New Orleans, LA 70118
U.S.A.
Tel. 1-504-865-5936; 1-504-865-5939
FAX: 1-504-865-6748
SAMPLE COURSES: Biblical and Common Law Approaches to Sin
Without Guilt, Civil Liberties in Israel and the United States, The
Legal Status of Women in Israel and the United States, Jewish Law

Ramat Can:

Widener University School of Law *
P.O. Box 7474
4601 Concord Pike
Wilmington, DE 19803
U.S.A.
Tel. 1-302-478-3000
FAX: 1-302-477-2282
SAMPLES COURSES: (Pending in 1990)

Tel Aviv:

Temple University *
School of Law
1719 North Broad Street
Philadelphia, PA 19122
U.S.A.
Tel. 1-215-787-7861
FAX: 1-215-787-1185
SAMPLE COURSES: Comparative Constitutional Law, Legal Aspects of the Middle East (Conflict and Resolution), Comparative
Criminal Law and Procedure

SPECIAL NOTES

U.S.A.

For an extensive and annually updated list of programs in international law sponsored by United States law schools around the world, see each year's January issue of the *Student Lawyer*, available through the American Bar Association, 750 North Lake Shore Drive, Chicago, Illinois, 60611, U.S.A.

EEC

For an extensive and annually updated list of summer courses offered in the European Community on European and International Law, see each year's May issue of the *Nouvelles Universitaires Européennes/European University News*, available through the Commission of the European Communities, University Information, 200 rue de la Loi, 1049 Brussels, BELGIUM, or through the offices of your local European Communities Delegation.

DIRECTORY OF ADVANCED DEGREE PROGRAMS IN INTERNATIONAL AND COMPARATIVE LAW WORLDWIDE

The following is a list of advanced degree programs worldwide,[1] as well as available fellowships and scholarships. The specific degrees available are noted where known. For more information, please contact the individual schools.

LIST OF COMMON ACRONYMS FOR ADVANCED DEGREES

B.C.L.	Bachelor of Civil Law
D.C.L.	Doctor of Comparative Law
D. Jur.	Doctor of Jurisprudence
D. Phil.	Doctor of Philosophy
Dr. iur.	Doctor of Jurisprudence
G.D.I.L.	Graduate Diploma in International Law
J.S.D.	Doctor of Juridical Science
J.S.M.	Master of the Science of Law
LL.D.	Doctor of Law
LL.M.	Master of Law
M.A.	Master of Arts
M.A.L.S.	Master of American Legal Studies
M.C.J.	Master of Comparative Jurisprudence
M.C.L.	Master of Comparative Law
M.E.L.S.	Master of European Legal Studies
M.I.C.L.	Master of International and Comparative Law
M.I.L.	Master of International Law
M.L.	Master of Law
M.L.I.	Master of Arts or Science in Legal Institutions
M. Litt.	Master of Letters
M. Phil.	Master of Philosophy
MM.L. & S.	Master of Marine Law and Science
Ph.D.	Doctor of Philosophy
S.J.D.	Doctor of Juridical Science; Doctor of Jurisprudence; Doctor of the Science of Law

---

1. For a study on the structural and functional aspects of the equivalence of degrees in the field, see *Comparability of Degrees and Diplomas in International Law*, by René Jean Dupuy and Gregory Tunkin, UNESCO, Paris, 1973. This publication is available through the United Nations Educational, Scientific and Cultural Organization (UNESCO), UNESCO House, 7, place Fontenay, 75007 Paris, FRANCE.

FELLOWSHIPS AND SCHOLARSHIPS

Robert Bosch Foundation Fellowship Program
Robert Bosch Stiftung GmbH
Heidehofstrasse 31
D-7000 Stuttgart 1
GERMANY
Tel. 49.711.46.08.40
FAX: 49.711.46.20.86

KEY ELEMENTS: A nine-month fellowship program in Germany. An advanced degree in a profession (including law), or the equivalent professional work experience, is required. Language training, travel and living expenses are paid. (The U.S. representative for the Robert Bosch Foundation Fellowship Program is CDS International, 330 Seventh Avenue, 19th Floor, New York, NY, 10001, U.S.A.; Tel. 1-212-760-1400; FAX: 1-212-268-1288.)

ERASMUS Bureau
rue d'Arlon 15
B-1040 Bruxelles
BELGIUM
Tel. 32.2.233.01.11
FAX: 32.2.233.01.50

KEY ELEMENTS: A comprehensive program of European Community financial support to EC Member State universities, their students and staff, for boosting student mobility and higher education cooperation throughout the European Community. ERASMUS student grants are for study abroad periods normally of 3-12 months' duration at a higher education institution in another Member State of the European Community. Interested students and university staff who are citizens of EC Member States should contact the ERASMUS office of their university for further information.

Fulbright Scholar Awards for Lecturing and Research Abroad
Council for International Exchange of Scholars (CIES)[2]
3400 International Drive, N.W.
Suite M-500
Washington, DC 20008
U.S.A.
Tel. 1-202-686-4000
FAX: 1-202-362-3442

KEY ELEMENTS: Offers 300 research and 700 university lecturing
opportunities in over 100 countries for postdoctoral candidates.

German Academic Exchange Service (DAAD)
Young Lawyers Program
Deutscher Akademischer Austauschdienst
Kennedyallee 50
D-5300 Bonn 2
GERMANY
Tel. 49.228.8821; 49.228.882.250
FAX: 49.228.882.444

KEY ELEMENTS: Ten-month program in German law for young
foreign lawyers, consisting of a two-month course in German legal
terminology at a German university, followed by a five-month course
organized by the North Rhine-Westphalian Ministry of Justice, and
a three-month internship. Scholarship includes tuition, fees, monthly
allowance, travel subsidy and health insurance. (New York branch
office of DAAD: 950 Third Avenue, 19th floor, New York, NY, 10022,
U.S.A.; Tel. 1-212-758-3223; FAX: 1-212-755-5780.)

Institute of International Education (IIE)[3]
309 United Nations Plaza
New York, NY 10017
U.S.A.
Tel. 1-212-883-8200
FAX: 1-212-984-5452

KEY ELEMENTS: Administers numerous private and public scholarship and fellowship programs worldwide for predoctoral and doctoral candidates.

---

2. This address for the Council for International Exchange of Scholars
(CIES) is for the headquarters office located in the United States. Interested
U.S. citizens should contact this office. Non-U.S. citizens interested in CIES
Fulbright programs should contact the United States Information Agency
(USIA) office of their local United States embassy or their country's local
Fulbright Commission.

3. This address for the Institute of International Education (IIE) is for the

International Human Rights Internship Program
Institute of International Education
1400 K Street, N.W.
Suite 650
Washington, DC 20005
U.S.A.
Tel. 1-202-682-6540
FAX: 1-202-842-1219

KEY ELEMENTS: Program seeks to promote the observance of the International Bill of Human Rights by strengthening and enhancing the development of human rights organizations through support of: (1) staff development opportunities, including exchanges and provision of specialized expertise; and, (2) training opportunities for individuals committed to human rights protection and promotion. Grants are given to staff members and volunteers of human rights organizations, as well as individuals who have demonstrated a commitment to human rights work, for training in such areas as documentation, reporting, use of international machineries, legal aid, medical work, human rights education and internal management. Grants may be used for different types of training opportunities, including the following: professional attachments; on-site training; study tours; and, training courses/seminars.

Jean Monnet Project
European Integration in University Studies
Commission of the European Communities
The Directorate General for Information, Communication
    and Culture
University Information Service
200, rue de la Loi
B-1049 Brussels
BELGIUM
Tel. 32.2.236.29.91; 32.2.235.63.36
FAX: 32.2.236.31.06

---

headquarters office located in the United States. Interested U.S. citizens should contact this office. Non-U.S. citizens interested in IIE programs should contact the local IIE educational advising center in their country. To purchase a complete directory of these educational advising centers, contact College Board Publications, Box 886, New York, New York, 10101, U.S.A. For a review of financial resources available for U.S citizens through IIE, see the latest edition of *Financial Resources for International Study*, available through Peterson's Guides, P.O. Box 2123, Princeton, New Jersey, 08543, U.S.A.

KEY ELEMENTS: Funds available to EC Member State universities and teachers for special educational projects concerning European integration; Jean Monnet Fellowships also available to both EC Member and non-Member State individuals for postdoctoral research in European integration at the European University Institute in Florence, Italy (see European University Institute entry on Advanced Degree Programs list in this *Guide*).

SPECIAL NOTES

A number of law schools offer their own graduate fellowships and scholarships for advanced degree programs. Check with the individual institutions for further information. A number of national and local governments also offer fellowships and scholarships to their citizens through officially-recognized grant-awarding bodies. Check with your local government officials for information on government-sponsored grants. Other organizations offering fellowship and scholarship programs for advanced legal studies include the following:

The Asia Foundation
465 California Street, 14th Floor
San Francisco, CA 94104
U.S.A.
(Mailing address: The Asia Foundation
                  P.O. Box 3223
                  San Francisco, CA 94119-3223
                  U.S.A.)

East-West Center
1777 East-West Road
Honolulu, HI 96822
U.S.A.

Director
International Affairs Program
The Ford Foundation
320 East 43rd Street
New York, NY 10017
U.S.A.

The Henry Luce Foundation, Inc.
111 West 50th Street
Room 3710
New York, NY 10020
U.S.A.

Max-Planck-Institut for
  European Law
Friedrichstrasse 2-6
D-6000 Frankfurt a.M.
GERMANY

Max-Planck-Institut for
  International Patent, Copyright
  and Competition Law
Siebertstrasse 3
D-8000 München 80
GERMANY

Max-Planck-Institut for
  International Penal Law
Günterstalstrasse 73
D-7800 Freiburg
GERMANY

Max-Planck-Institut for
  International Private Law
Mittelweg 187
D-2000 Hamburg 13
GERMANY

Max-Planck-Intitut for
  International Public Law
Berliner Strasse 48
D-6900 Heidelberg 1
GERMANY

Max-Planck-Institut for
  International Social Law
Leopoldstrasse 24
D-8000 München 40
GERMANY

OAS Fellowships
Department of Fellowships and Training
Organization of American States
1889 F Street, N.W.
Washington, DC 20006-4499
U.S.A.

Rotary International
The Rotary Foundation
One Rotary Center
1560 Sherman Avenue
Evanston, IL 60201
U.S.A.

For a review of American-sponsored programs designed to facil-
itate the entry into or advancement in careers in international
law, international affairs, and public policy, see *International Law,
International Affairs, and Public Policy: A Fellowship-Internship-
Scholarship Guide*, Rachel de la Vega, ed., American Society of
International Law, 1991. This 20-page booklet, which is based on
a 1990 report by Leslie McKnight Yates to the Society's project
on Women and Minorities in International Law, and which contains a section on programs offered specifically for minorities, can
be ordered through the American Society of International Law,
2223 Massachusetts Avenue, N.W., Washington, D.C., 20008-2864,
U.S.A.

ADVANCED DEGREE PROGRAMS
IN INTERNATIONAL AND COMPARATIVE LAW

Note: This list includes law schools offering advanced degree programs in international and comparative law, or advanced degree programs in domestic law open to foreign law students. Some schools listed offer general advanced degree programs, with a concentration of studies available in the area. We have attempted to list as many advanced degree programs as possible which may be of particular interest to the international practitioner. Some schools which are not listed, which offer advanced degree programs in domestic law, may admit foreign law students on a case-by-case basis. For admissions policies at these institutions, contact the individual schools.

AFRICA

Algeria

Note: Algeria follows the French model for advanced degrees; please refer to the entry for France for further information.

Université d'Alger
Faculté de droit
2, rue Didouche Mouran
Algers
ALGERIA

Université d'Oran
Faculté de droit
Boîte postale 1524
Es-Senia, Oran
ALGERIA

Kenya

> University of Nairobi
> POB 30197
> Nairobi
> KENYA
> Ph.D., LL.M.—International Law

Morocco

Note: Morocco follows the French model for advanced degrees;
please refer to the entry for France for further information.

> Université Sidi Mohammed Ben Abdellah
> Faculté de droit
> BP 452
> Dhar El Mahraz
> Fes
> MOROCCO

> Université Mohammed V
> Faculté de droit
> BP 554
> 3, rue Michlifen
> Agdal, Rabat
> MOROCCO

Nigeria

> University of Lagos Law School
> Akoka, Yaba
> Lagos
> NIGERIA
> LL.M.—International Law

Tanzania

> University of Dar-es-Salaam
> POB 35091
> Dar-es-Salaam
> TANZANIA
> Ph.D., LL.M.

Tunisia

Note: Tunisia follows the French model for advanced degrees;
please refer to the entry for France for further information.

Université de Tunis (I & II)
Ministère de l'Education, de l'Enseignement
    Supérieur, et de la Recherche Scientifique
rue Ouled Haffouz
Tunis
TUNISIA

ASIA

People's Republic of China

Graduate School
Chinese Academy of Social Sciences
Beijing
PEOPLE'S REPUBLIC OF CHINA
LL.M.

Graduate School
Chinese University of Law and Politics
41 Xueyuan Road
Beijing
PEOPLE'S REPUBLIC OF CHINA
LL.M., LL.D.

Graduate School
East China College of Law and Politics
1575 Wanhangdu Road
Shanghai
PEOPLE'S REPUBLIC OF CHINA
LL.M.

International Law Institute
College of Foreign Affairs
24 Zhanlan Road
Beijing
PEOPLE'S REPUBLIC OF CHINA
LL.M.

Department of International Economic Law
University of Foreign Economy and Trade
Andingmenwai Xiaoguan
Beijing
PEOPLE'S REPUBLIC OF CHINA
LL.M., LL.D.

Fudan University
Faculty of Law
220 Handan Road
Shanghai
PEOPLE'S REPUBLIC OF CHINA
M.A.

Department of Law
Jilin University
Jie Fang Road
Changchun City, Jilin Province
PEOPLE'S REPUBLIC OF CHINA
LL.M.

Department of Law
Nankai University
94 Weijin Road
Tianjin
PEOPLE'S REPUBLIC OF CHINA
LL.M.

Peking University
Institute of International Law
Hai Dian, Beijing
PEOPLE'S REPUBLIC OF CHINA
M.A.—International Law; LL.M., LL.D. available
   through Law Department

People's University of China
Faculty of Law
39 Haidian Road
Beijing
PEOPLE'S REPUBLIC OF CHINA
LL.M.

Institute of Law
Shanghai Academy of Social Sciences
Shanghai
PEOPLE'S REPUBLIC OF CHINA
LL.M.

Department of International Economic Law
Shanghai College of Foreign Trade
Shanghai
PEOPLE'S REPUBLIC OF CHINA
M.A.—International Law

Department of International Shipping
Shanghai Shipping College
1550 Pudong Dadao
Shanghai
PEOPLE'S REPUBLIC OF CHINA
LL.M.

Wuhan University
Institute of International Law
Luojia Mt.
Wuhan City, Hubei Province
PEOPLE'S REPUBLIC OF CHINA
M.A.—International Law; LL.M., LL.D. available
   through Law Department

Department of Law
Xiamen [Amoy] University
Xiamen City
Fujian Province
PEOPLE'S REPUBLIC OF CHINA
LL.M.—International Economic Law; LL.D.

Department of Law
Zhongshan University
Henan Kang Le Yuan
Guangzhou City
Guangdong Province
PEOPLE'S REPUBLIC OF CHINA
LL.M.—International Law

Hong Kong

University of Hong Kong
Faculty of Law
4/F Leung Building
Pokfulam Road
HONG KONG
LL.M.—International Trade, Transport, Commercial Law,
Law of China

India

Dean
Faculty of Law
University of Delhi
Delhi 110 007
INDIA
M.L.I. (international courses held, in part, in conjuction with
the Indian Academy of International Law and Diplomacy)

Centre for Studies in Diplomacy, International Law
and Economics
School of International Studies
Jawaharial Nehru University
New Mehrauli Road
New Delhi 110 067
INDIA
M.Phil., Ph.D., LL.M.—International Law

University of Madras
Department of International Law
and Constitutional Law
Chepauk
Triplicane PO
Madras 600 005
INDIA
M.L.—International Law and Constitutional Law

Department of Law (P.G. Studies)
University of Mysore
Mysore (Karnataka State)
INDIA
LL.M.—International Law

P.G. Department of Law
University of Nagpur
Nagpur (Maharastra State)
INDIA
LL.M.—International Law

Department of Legal Studies
Srivenkateswara University
Tirupathi (Andhra Pradesh State)
INDIA
M.L.—International Law and Constitutional Law

Japan

Graduate School of Law
Chuo University
742-1 Higashinakano,
Hachioji-shi
Tokyo 192-03
JAPAN
Master's degree; Doctorate (Anglo-American Law,
    Criminal Law, Civil Law, Public Law)

Graduate School of Law
Doshisha University
Imadegawa-dori, Karasuma-Higashiiru,
Kamigyo-ku, Kyoto-shi
Kyoto 602
JAPAN
Master's degree; Doctorate (Private Law, Public Law)

Graduate School of Law
Hitotsubasi University
2-1 NaKa, Kunitachi-shi
Tokyo 186
JAPAN
Master's degree; Doctorate (Law and Economy,
    Law and State)

Graduate School of Law
Hokkaido University
Nishi 5, Kita 8,
Kita-ku, Sapporo-shi
Hokkaido 060
JAPAN
Master's degree; Doctorate (Private Law, Public Law)

Graduate School of Law
Keio University
2-15-45 Mita, Minato-ku
Tokyo 108
JAPAN
Master's degree; Doctorate (Civil Law, Public Law)

Graduate School of Law
Kyoto University
Yoshida Honmachi,
Sakyo-ku, Kyoto-shi
Kyoto 606
JAPAN
Master's degree; Doctorate (Basic Law,
   Private and Criminal Law, Public Law)

Graduate School of Law
Kyushu University
6-10-1 Hakozaki, Higasi-ku
Fukuoka-shi
Fukuoka 812
JAPAN
Master's degree; Doctorate (Judicial Law, Legal Theory,
   Public Law, Social Law)

Admissions Committee for Legal Studies
Graduate School of Law
Meijo University
1-501 Shiogamaguchi, Tempaku-ku
Nagoya 468
JAPAN
LL.M.—Public and Private International Law

Graduate School of Law
Nagoya University
Furo-cho, Chikusa-ku,
Nagoya-shi
Aichi 464
JAPAN
Master's degree; Doctorate (Public Law,
    Civil and Criminal Law)

Graduate School of Law
Osaka University
1-1 Yamadaoka, Suita-shi
Osaka 565
JAPAN
Master's degree; Doctorate (Civil Law, Public Law)

Graduate School of Law
Rikkyo (St. Paul's) University
3-34-1 Nishi Ikebukuro,
Toshima-ku
Tokyo 171
JAPAN
Master's degree; Doctorate (Civil and Criminal Law,
    Comparative Law)

Graduate School of Law
Tohoku University
2-1-1 Katahira, Sendai-shi
Miyagi 980
JAPAN
Master's degree; Doctorate (Foundations of Law,
    Private Law, Public Law)

Graduate School of Law and Politics
The University of Tokyo
7-3-1 Hongo,
Bunkyo-ku
Tokyo 113
JAPAN
Master's degree; Doctorate (Basic Science of Law, Civil and
    Criminal Law, Public Law)

Graduate School of Law
Waseda University
1-6-1 Nishi-Waseda,
Shinjuku-ku
Tokyo 160
JAPAN
Master's degree; Doctorate (Civil Law, Fundamental Legal
   Studies, Public Law)

Republic of Korea

Graduate Law Programs
Faculty of Law
University of Korea
Seoul 136
REPUBLIC OF KOREA

Graduate Law Programs
Seoul National University
College of Law
Seoul 151
REPUBLIC OF KOREA

Graduate Law Programs
Yonsei University
134 Shinchon-dong
Sudaemoon-ku
Seoul 120
REPUBLIC OF KOREA

Sri Lanka

University of Colombo
Faculty of Law
94 Cumaratunga Munidasa Mawatha
P.O. Box 1490
Colombo 3
SRI LANKA
LL.M.—International Law; Diploma in International
   Trade Law and Practice; Ph.D. in Research

Taiwan

Graduate Program of Law
Tunghai University
Taichung
TAIWAN
LL.M.—International and Domestic Law, Comparative Law;
  Graduate Program of Politics: LL.M.—International
  Law and Politics

Graduate Program of Law
National Chengchi University
64 Chih-nan Road
Sec. 2, Wen-shan Dist.
Taipei
TAIWAN
LL.M.—International and Domestic Law, Comparative Law;
  Graduate Program of Politics: LL.M.—International
  Law and Politics

Graduate School of Law
Chinese Culture University
55 Hua-kang Road
Yangming Shan
Taipei
TAIWAN
LL.M.—International and Domestic Law, Comparative Law;
  Graduate School of Politics: LL.M.—International Law
  and Politics; *Graduate Program of Sino-American
  Relations*: LL.M.—area studies

Graduate School of Law
National Chunghsing University
69, Sec. 2
Chian-kuo N. Road
Taipei
TAIWAN
LL.M.—International and Domestic Law, Comparative Law;
  Graduate School of Politics: LL.M.—International Law
  and Politics

Graduate Program of Law
Soochow University
56 Kuei-yang Street
Sec. 1,
Taipei
TAIWAN
LL.M.—International and Domestic Law, Comparative Law;
  Graduate Program of Politics: LL.M.—International
  Law and Politics

Graduate Program in Law
National Taiwan University
21 Hsuchow Road
Taipei
TAIWAN
LL.M.—International and Domestic Law, Comparative Law;
  Graduate Program of Politics: LL.M.—International
  Law and Politics

Graduate Institute of International Affairs and
   Strategic Studies
Tamkang University
18 Li-shui Street
Taipei
TAIWAN
LL.M.—International Law and Politics; *Graduate Institutes
  of American Culture and European Studies*:
  LL.M.—area studies

Graduate Program of Law
Fu Jen Catholic University
Hsin Chuang
Taipei County
TAIWAN
LL.M.—International and Domestic Law, Comparative Law;
  Graduate Program of Politics: LL.M.—International
  Law and Politics

AUSTRALASIA

Australia

Assistant Registrar
Office of the Registrar
University of Adelaide
Box 498 GPO
Adelaide, South Australia 5001
AUSTRALIA
LL.M., Ph.D.

Registrar
Office of the Registrar
Australian National University
GPO Box 4
Canberra ACT 2601
AUSTRALIA
M.I.L., G.D.I.L.—International Law

Program Manager
Graduate Studies and Continuing Education
The University of Melbourne
Faculty of Law
Parkville, Victoria 3052
AUSTRALIA
Ph.D., LL.D., LL.M.—International and Comparative Law
   (among others); Graduate Diplomas in Asian Law,
   Government Law, Intellectual Property Law and Labour
   Relations Law

Secretary
Graduate Studies Programme
Faculty of Law
Monash University
Clayton, Victoria 3168
AUSTRALIA
Ph.D., LL.M., G.D.I.L.—International and Comparative
   Law (among others)

Malaysia

> Universiti Malaya
> Faculty of Law
> Lembah Pantai
> 59100 Kuala Lumpur
> MALAYSIA
> LL.M., M.C.L.

New Zealand

> University of Auckland
> Faculty of Law
> Private Bag
> Auckland 1
> NEW ZEALAND
>
> Faculty of Law
> Victoria University of Wellington
> P.O. Box 600
> Wellington
> NEW ZEALAND
> International and comparative law degrees

Singapore

> Graduate Law Programmes
> National University of Singapore
> Faculty of Law
> 10 Kent Ridge Crescent
> SINGAPORE 0511
> Ph.D., LL.M.—Constitutional Law (by thesis or coursework)

EUROPE

Note: For more information on individual law schools in the European Community, see *Higher Education in the European Community: Student Handbook*, available through the Office for Official Publications of the European Communities, 2, rue Mercier, L-2985 LUXEMBOURG, or through the offices of your local European Communities Delegation. A parallel publication covering higher education in the member countries of the Council of Europe is also available through the Council of Europe, Publications and Documents Division, BP 431/R6, 67006 Strasbourg Cedex, FRANCE.

Austria

Institut für Völkerrecht und
  Internationale Beziehungen
Universität zu Wien
Universitätsstrasse 2
A-1090 Wien
AUSTRIA
Diploma of the Program of International Studies

Belgium

College of Europe
Dyver 11
B-8000 Brugge
BELGIUM
M.E.L.S., Ph.D.; Diploma of Advanced European Legal
  Studies

Vrije Universiteit Brussel
Faculty of Law
Program on International Legal Cooperation (PILC)
Pleinlaan 2
1050 Brussels
BELGIUM
M.I.C.L. (in English)

Université Libre de Bruxelles
Institut d'Etudes Européennes
avenue Franklin Roosevelt 39, Boîte 5
B-1050 Bruxelles
BELGIUM
Licence Spéciale en Droit Européen

Université Libre de Bruxelles
Faculté de droit
avenue Paul Heger 2
Bâtiment H
B-1050 Bruxelles
BELGIUM
Licence Spéciale en Droit Comparé

Katholieke Universiteit Leuven
Faculty of Law
Naamsestraat 22
B-3000 Leuven
BELGIUM
LL.M.—European Law (in English)

France

Note: Most universities in France offer graduate degree diplomas
in Public Law, Private Law, and Law and Political Economy. Among the specialized areas offered are: International
Law (Public and Private), Civil Law, Law and Economics,
Legal History, and Criminal Science. These degrees consist
of the D.E.S. (Diplôme d'Etudes Supérieures), D.E.A.
(Diplôme d'Etudes Approfondies) and D.E.S.S. (Diplôme
d'Etudes des Sciences Spécialisées). Almost all principal
universities also offer a "Doctorat de 3ème Cycle" or a
"Doctorat d'Etat." The schools listed below are provided for
illustrative purposes only.

Université de droit, d'économie et des sciences
(Aix-Marseille III)
Faculté de droit
Service de Documentation
3, avenue Robert Schuman
13621 Aix-en-Provence
FRANCE

Université de Bordeaux I
Faculté de droit
351, cours de la Libération
33405 Talence Cedex
FRANCE

Université de Caen
Faculté de droit
Esplanade de la Paix
14032 Caen Cedex
FRANCE

Université de Clermont-Ferrand I
Faculté de droit
49, boulevard Gergovia
Boîte postale 32
63001 Clermont-Ferrand
FRANCE

Université de Bourgogne (Dijon)
Faculté de droit
Campus universitaire de Montmuzard
Boîte postale 138
21004 Dijon Cedex
FRANCE
D.E.A.—droit de l'économie

Université de Grenoble II
Université des sciences sociales
U.E.R. des Sciences Juridiques
Domaine universitaire
Saint-Martin-d'Hères
Boîte postale 47X
38040 Grenoble Cedex
FRANCE

Université de droit et de la santé (Lille II)
Faculté de droit
42, rue Paul Duez
59800 Lille
FRANCE
LL.M., D.E.A., D.E.S.S.—droit international

Université de Lyon II
Faculté de droit
86, rue Pasteur
69365 Lyon Cedex 2
FRANCE

Université Jean Moulin (Lyon III)
Faculté de droit
1, rue de l'Université
Lyon 7ᵉ
Boîte postale 0638
69339 Lyon Cedex 02
FRANCE
D.E.A., D.E.S.S.

Université de Montpellier I
Faculté de droit
5, boulevard Henri IV
Boîte postale 1017
34006 Montpellier Cedex
FRANCE

Université de Nancy II
Faculté de droit
25, rue Baron Louis
Boîte postale 454
54001 Nancy Cedex
FRANCE

Institute of the Law of
  Peace and Development
7, avenue Robert Schuman
06050 Nice Cedex
FRANCE
D.E.A., Ph.D.—droit international

Université de Nice
Faculté de droit
Parc Valrose
06034 Nice Cedex
FRANCE

Université Panthéon-Sorbonne (Paris I)
Faculté de droit
12, place du Panthéon
75231 Paris Cedex 05
FRANCE

Université de droit,
    d'économie et de sciences sociales (Paris II)
Faculté des sciences
    juridiques
12, place du Panthéon
75231 Paris Cedex 05
FRANCE

Université de Poitiers
Faculté de droit
15, rue de Blossac
86034 Poitiers Cedex
FRANCE

Université de Rennes I
Faculté de droit
2, rue du Thabor
35000 Rennes
FRANCE

Université des science humaines (Strasbourg II)
22, rue Descartes
67084 Strasbourg Cedex
FRANCE

Université des sciences juridiques,
    politiques, sociales et de
    technologie (Université Robert Schuman/Strasbourg III)
place d'Athènes
67084 Strasbourg Cedex
FRANCE

Université des sciences sociales (Toulouse I)
place Anatole France
31042 Toulouse Cedex
FRANCE
D.E.A.—droit économique international; D.E.S.S.—droit
    international

Université Paul Sabatier (Toulouse III)
Faculté de droit
118, route de Narbonne
31062 Toulouse Cedex
FRANCE

Germany

(University of Bonn)
Graduate Law Programs
Rechts- und Staatswissenschaftliche Fakultät
  der Friedrich-Wilhelms-Universität Bonn
Adenaueralle 24 - 42
D-5300 Bonn 1
GERMANY
M.C.L. (Magister der Rechtsvergleichung), Dr. iur.

(University of Freiburg)
Graduate Law Programs
Rechtswissenschaftliche Fakultät
  der Universität Freiburg
Europaplatz
D-7800 Freiburg
GERMANY
LL.M. (Legum Magister), Dr. iur.
  (for applications, contact Akademisches Auslandsamt der
  Universität Freiburg, Heinrich-von-Stephan-Strasse 25,
  D-7800 Freiburg, GERMANY)

(University of Giessen)
Fachbereich Rechtswissenschaft
  der Justus-Liebig-Universität Giessen
Licher Strasse 72
D-6300 Giessen
GERMANY
LL.M. (Magister Iuris), Dr. iur.

(University of Göttingen)
Juristisches Seminar
  der Georg-August-Universität Göttingen
Platz der Göttinger Sieben 6
D-3400 Göttingen
GERMANY
LL.M. (Magister Iuris), Dr. iur.

(Fern University of Hagen)
Rechtswissenschaftliche Facultät der
  Hagen Fernuniversität
Konkorddiastrasse 5
D-5800 Hagen
GERMANY
LL.M. (Magister), Dr. iur.

(University of Heidelberg)
Juristische Fakultät der
  Ruprecht-Karls-Universität
Friedrich-Ebert-Anlage 6 - 10
D-6900 Heidelberg 1
GERMANY
LL.M. (Legum Magister), Dr. iur.

(University of Kiel)
An den Prasidenten der
  Christian-Albrechts-Universität zu Kiel
Akademisches Auslandsamt
Olshausenstrasse 40
D-2300 Kiel
GERMANY
LL.M. (Magister Legum), Dr. iur.

(University of Mainz)
Rechtswissenschaftliche Facultät der
  Universität Mainz
Postfach 39 80
D-6500 Mainz
GERMANY
LL.M. (Magister), Dr. iur.

(University of Mannheim)
Fakultät für Rechtswissenschaft der
  Universität Mannheim
Schloss, Westflugel
D-6800 Mannheim
GERMANY
LL.M. (Legum Magister), Dr. iur.

(University of Münster)
Rechtswissenschaftliche Fakultät der
  Westfälischen Wilhelms-Universität Münster
Universitätsstrasse 14/16
D-4400 Münster
GERMANY
LL.M. (Magister Legum), Dr. iur.

(University of Passau)
Rechtswissenschaftliche Fakultät der
  Universität Passau
Innstrasse 40
D-8390 Passau
GERMANY
LL.M. (Magister), Dr. iur.

(University of Regensburg)
Juristische Fakultät der
  Universität Regensburg
Universitätsstrasse 31
D-8400 Regensburg 1
GERMANY
LL.M. (Magister Legum), Dr. iur.

(University of Saarbrücken)
Rechtswissenschaftliche Fakultät der
  Universität Saarbrücken
Im Stadtwald
D-6600 Saarbrücken 11
GERMANY
License (Lizentiatenprufung)

(University of Trier)
Fachbereich Rechtswissenschaft der
  Universität Trier
Tarforst
Gebäude C
D-5500 Trier
GERMANY
LL.M. (Magister der Recht), Dr. iur.
  (for applications, contact Akademisches Auslandsamt
  der Universität Trier, Postfach 3825, D-5500 Trier,
  GERMANY)

(University of Tubingen)
Juristische Fakultät der
  Universität Tübingen
Wilhelmstrasse 7
D-7400 Tübingen
GERMANY
LL.M. (Legum Magister), Dr. iur.

(University of Würzburg)
Rechtswissenschaftliche Fakultät der
  Universität Würzburg
Sanderring 2
D-8700 Würzburg
GERMANY
LL.M. (Magister), Dr. iur.

Ireland

University College
Faculty of Law
Belfield
Dublin 4
IRELAND
M.A.

Italy

Note: Each university in Italy offers a "Dottore in Giurisprudenza" (minimum four-year program) and graduate diplomas
in specialized programs (including international law). A
"Dottorato di Ricerca" (limited number issued; open to Italian citizens only) is also available by competition. The schools
listed below offer special degrees other than those mentioned, or are provided for illustrative purposes only.

Collegio Europeo di Parma
Borgo Lalatta 14
43100 Parma
ITALY
Certificate in Law and Economics
  of the European Communities

European University Institute
Academic Service
Badia Fiesolana
5 via dei Roccettini
50016 San Domenico di Fiesole
(Firenze)
ITALY
Ph.D, LL.M.—Comparative, European, and International Law

Universita Degli Studi di Firenze
Facoltà di Giurisprudenza
Via Giusti 7
50121 Firenze
ITALY

Universita Degli Studi di Roma—'la Sapienza'
Facoltà di Giurisprudenza
Citta Universitaria
00100 Roma
ITALY

The Netherlands

Europa Instituut
Universiteit van Amsterdam
Herengracht, 508
1002 Amsterdam
THE NETHERLANDS
Doctoraat

University of Amsterdam
School for Executive Development
   in International Relations (ASEDIR)
Oudezijds Achterburgwal 237
1012 DL Amsterdam
THE NETHERLANDS
Diploma in Law of the European Communities

The Hague Academy of International Law
Peace Palace
Carnegieplein 2
2517 KJ The Hague
THE NETHERLANDS
Diploma in International Law (by examination)

Rijksuniversiteit te Leiden
Hugo de Grootstraat 27
2311 XK Leiden
THE NETHERLANDS
Doctoraat; Diploma in European Law; Certificates in International, European, and Comparative Law; Ph.D. (Promotie) (courses conducted in English)

European Studies Program
Tilburg University
Hogeschoollaan 225
P.O. Box 90153
5000 LE Tilburg
THE NETHERLANDS
Diploma in European Law

Rijksuniversiteit te Utrecht
Janskerkhof, 3
5512 BK Utrecht
THE NETHERLANDS
Doctoraat; Diploma in European Law; Certificates in European Law, Human Rights, Comparative Law, International Law and Relations, International Law and Economics, and Law of the Sea; Ph.D. (Promotie) (courses conducted in English)

Spain

Note: Master's degrees and doctorates concentrating in international law are available from all faculties of law in Spain. The schools listed below are provided for illustrative purposes only.

Universidad de Barcelona
Facultad de Derecho
Gran Via de les
   Corts Catalanes 585
08007 Barcelona
SPAIN

Universidad Autónoma de Madrid
Facultad de Derecho
Carretera de Colmenar Viejo
km 15
Cantoblanco
28071 Madrid
SPAIN

Universidad de Salamanca
Facultad de Derecho
Patio de Escuelas 1
37071 Salamanca
SPAIN

Universidad de Valladolid
Facultad de Derecho
Cárcel 6
47071 Valladolid
SPAIN

Sweden

Assistant to the Dean
    of International Studies
Faculty of Law
Stockholm University
106 91 Stockholm
SWEDEN
M.C.L., M.I.L., Diploma in Graduate Legal Studies

Switzerland

The Graduate Institute of International Studies
P.O. Box 36
132, rue de Lausanne
1211 Geneva 21
SWITZERLAND
Diploma of Higher Studies; Ph.D.; Certificate; License in International History and Politics, International Economics, and International Law

Turkey

Avrupa Hukuk Arastirma ve Egitim Merkezi
(Center for Research and Study of European Law)
Hukuk Fakultesi
Beyazit
Istanbul
TURKEY

United Kingdom *(England and Wales)*

Graduate Law Programmes
Buckingham University
Buckingham MK18 1EG
ENGLAND

Secretary
Board of Graduate Studies
University of Cambridge
4 Mill Lane
Cambridge CB2 1RZ
ENGLAND
Diploma in International Law; LL.M., M.Litt, Ph.D.

Graduate Law Programmes
Kent University
Canterbury CT2 7NZ
ENGLAND

Dean
University of Essex
Faculty of Law
Wivenhoe Park
Colchester, Essex CO4 3SQ
ENGLAND
LL.M.—Human Rights Law;
   M.Phil.; Ph.D.—International Law

Secretary of Facilities
University of Exeter
Northcote House
The Queen's Drive
Exeter EX4 4QJ
ENGLAND
M.E.L.S.; LL.M.—International
   Business Law; M.Phil.; Ph.D.—
   International Law

Center for European Legal Studies
Faculty of Law
University of Exeter
Amory Building
Rennes Drive
Exeter EX4 4RJ
ENGLAND
M.A.

Faculty of Law
University of Hull
Hull HU6 7RX
ENGLAND
Ph.D., LL.M., M.Phil.—
   International Law; Diploma in International
   Business Law

University of Leeds
Faculty of Law
Leeds LS2 9JT
ENGLAND
M.A.

Graduate Law Programmes
Liverpool University
PO Box 147
Liverpool L69 3BX
ENGLAND
Diploma in International Law

Graduate Law Programmes
London School of Economics
University of London
Houghton Street
London WC2A 2AE
ENGLAND
Diploma in International Law; LL.M., M.Phil., Ph.D.

Graduate Law Programmes
Queen Mary College
University of London
Mile End Road
London E1 4NS
ENGLAND
Diploma in Intellectual Property Law

The Director
Centre for Islamic & Middle East Law (CIMEL)
School of Oriental and African Studies
University of London
Thornhaugh Street
Russell Square
London WC1H 0XG
ENGLAND

Graduate Law Programmes
University College
University of London
Gower Street
London WC1E 6BT
ENGLAND
Diploma in International Law; Diploma
   in International Business Law; Diploma in Shipping Law;
   Certificate in Air and Space Law

Postgraduate Secretary
University of Manchester
Faculty of Law
Manchester M13 9PL
ENGLAND
Ph.D., M.Phil.; Diploma in International Law

Division of Law
University of Brunel
Uxbridge
Middlesex UB8 3PH
ENGLAND
M.A.

Graduate Law Programmes
Nottingham University
University Park
Nottingham NG7 2RD
ENGLAND

Registrar's Office
University of Oxford
Wellington Square
Oxford OX1 2JD
ENGLAND
B.C.L., M.Litt, D.Phil

Graduate Law Programmes
University College of Wales—
   Aberystwyth
King Street
Aberystwyth SY23 2AX
WALES
Diploma in International Law
   and Relations; Diploma in European
   Law and Government

Graduate Law Programmes
University of Wales College—
   Cardiff
PO Box 68
Cardiff CF1 3XA
WALES

United Kingdom *(Scotland)*

University of Edinburgh
Faculty of Law
Old College
South Bridge
Edinburgh EH8 9YL
SCOTLAND
LL.M.—Public International Law

Department of European Law
University of Glasgow
Glasgow G12 8QQ
SCOTLAND
M.A.

LATIN AMERICA/CARIBBEAN

Argentina

Director
Instituto de Investigación y Post Grado
Universidad Austral
Vincente Lopez 1950
Capital Federal (Buenos Aires)
ARGENTINA

Director del Departamento de Estudios para Graduados
Universidad de Buenos Aires
Facultad de Derecho y Ciencias Sociales
Figueroa Alcorto y Pueyredón
Capital Federal (Buenos Aires)
ARGENTINA
Doctorate degree in International Law

Universidad Nacional de Rosario
Córdoba 1814
2000 Rosario
ARGENTINA
Master's degree—Foreign Commerce (directed to
persons with a legal backround)

Brazil

Instituto de Rio Branco
Universidade de Brasilia
Agencia Postale 15
70910 Brasilia, DF
BRAZIL
Degree program in International Relations, including
  International Law

Chile

Instituto de Estudios Internacionales
Universidad de Chile
Condell 249
Santiago
CHILE
Master's degree; Diploma—International Law and Relations

Instituto de Ciencias Politicas
Pontificia Universidad Catolica de Chile
Casa Central Alameda 4o piso
Santiago
CHILE
Master's degree in Political Science with concentration in
  International Law and Relations

Colombia

Universidad de los Andes
Carrera 1A, No. 18-A-70
APDO Aéreo 4976
Bogota
COLOMBIA

Universidad Externado de Colombia
Facultad de Comercio
Calle 12, Nos. 1-17 Este
APDO Aéreo 034141
Bogota
COLOMBIA

Mexico

Universidad Nacional Autonoma de Mexico
Facultad de Derecho
Ciudad Universitaria
Del. Coyoacan
04510 Mexico, DF
MEXICO
Ph.D. — International Law; M.I.L.

Peru

Centro Peruano de Estudios Internacionales
Pontificia Universidad Catolica de Peru
Avenida La Paz No. 1580
Miraflores
Lima 19
PERU
Master's degree — International Economic Law

Puerto Rico

Catholic University of Puerto Rico
School of Law
Ponce, PR 00732
U.S.A.
Spanish doctorate in Civil Law (in cooperation
   with Valladolid University, Spain);
   LL.M. — Comparative Law (courses
   conducted in Spanish)

MIDDLE EAST

Egypt

Note: Each University in Egypt offers a "Doctorate" and a
"Superior Diploma in International Law." The schools listed
below are provided for illustrative purposes only.

Ain Shams University
Faculty of Law
Kasr-El-Zaafaran
Abbasiya
Cairo
EGYPT

University of Alexandria
Faculty of Law
22 El-Geish Avenue
El-Shatby, Alexandria
EGYPT

University of Assiut
Faculty of Law
Assiut
EGYPT
(also offers a "Superior Diploma in Human Rights")

University of Cairo
Faculty of Law
Orman, Giza
Cairo
EGYPT

Israel

Hebrew University of Jerusalem
Faculty of Law
Mount Scopus
91905 Jerusalem
ISRAEL
D.Jur., LL.M.

Tel Aviv University
Faculty of Law
Ramat-Aviv
69978 Tel Aviv
ISRAEL
Doctorate in International Law

Syria

Note: Syria follows the French model for advanced degrees; please refer to the entry for France for further information.

University of Damascus
Faculty of Law
Damascus
SYRIA

NORTH AMERICA

Canada

Graduate Law Programmes
University of British Columbia
Faculty of Law
1822 East Mall
Vancouver, British Columbia
CANADA V6T 1Y1

Secretary
Graduate Studies
Faculty of Law
Dalhousie University
6061 University Avenue
Halifax, Nova Scotia
CANADA B3H 4H9
LL.M., J.S.D.

Université Laval
Faculté de Droit
Sainte-Foy, Quebec
CANADA G1K 7P4

Institute of Air and Space Law and Institute of
    Comparative Law
McGill University
3644 Peel Street
Room #15
Montreal, Quebec
CANADA H3A 1W9

Université de Montréal
Faculté de Droit
C.P. 6128, Succursale A
Montréal, Quebec
CANADA H3C 3J7

Graduate Law Programmes
University of Ottawa
Faculty of Law
57 Louis Pasteur
Ottawa, Ontario
CANADA K1N 6N5

Graduate Law Programmes
Queens University
Faculty of Law
Kingston, Ontario
CANADA K7L 3N6

Associate Dean
Graduate Studies
Faculty of Law
University of Toronto
78 Queen's Park
Toronto, Ontario
CANADA M5J 2C5
LL.M., S.J.D.—International Trade
   and Business Law

United States

Note: For more information on individual law schools in the United
   States, see the *Official Guide to U.S. Law Schools*, available
   through the *Law School Admission Council*, Law Services,
   Box 63, Newtown, PA, 18940-0063, U.S.A.; Tel. 1-215-968-
   1111; FAX: 1-215-968-1119; or, contact the *Section of Legal
   Education and Admissions to the Bar of the American Bar
   Association*, 750 North Lake Shore Drive, Chicago, IL, 60611,
   U.S.A.; Tel. 1-312-988-5581; FAX: 1-312-988-6281.

Director of the M.C.L. Program
Admissions Office
University of Alabama
School of Law
101 Paul Bryant Drive East
Box 1435
Tuscaloosa, AL 35401
U.S.A.
M.C.L.

Graduate International Legal
   Studies Program
American University
Washington College of Law
4400 Massachusetts Avenue, N.W.
Washington, DC 20016
U.S.A.
LL.M.—International Law

Director of the M.C.L. Degree Program
California Western School of Law
350 Cedar Street
San Diego, CA 92101
U.S.A.
M.C.L.

Admissions Office
University of California at Berkeley
Boalt Hall School of Law
Berkeley, CA 94720
U.S.A.
LL.M., J.S.D.

Admissions Office
University of California at Los Angeles
School of Law
405 Hilgard Avenue
Los Angeles, CA 90024-1476
U.S.A.
LL.M. (for non-United States law school graduates only);
LL.M. (two-year program)—Teaching Public International
Law and Institutions (for minority and women scholars)

Catholic University of Puerto Rico
School of Law
Ponce, PR 00732
U.S.A.
Spanish doctorate in Civil Law (in cooperation
  with Valladolid University, Spain); LL.M.—Comparative
  Law (courses conducted in Spanish)

Graduate Student Affairs
University of Chicago
Law School
1111 East 60th Street
Chicago, IL 60637
U.S.A.
D.C.L., M.C.L., J.S.D.; LL.M.—
  International Law (for non-United States law school
  graduates only)

Columbia University
School of Law
Graduate Legal Studies
435 West 116th Street
New York, NY 10027
U.S.A.
J.S.D., LL.M.—International and Comparative Law
  (among others)

Dickinson School of Law
150 College Street
Carlisle, PA 17013
U.S.A.
M.C.L.

Graduate Law Programs
Fordham University
School of Law
140 West 62nd Street
New York, NY 10023
U.S.A.
LL.M.—International Business and Trade Law

Dean of Admissions
William S. Richardson
School of Law
University of Hawaii at Manoa
2515 Dole Street
Honolulu, HI 96822
  M.C.L./LL.M.—Pacific and Asian Legal Studies
  (program in formation as of 1990)

Director, Post-J.D. Programs
George Washington University
National Law Center
2000 H Street, N.W.
Washington, DC 20052
U.S.A.
LL.M.—International Law;
  M.C.L.

Graduate Admissions Coordinator
Georgetown University
Law Center
600 New Jersey Avenue, N.W.
Washington, DC 20001
U.S.A.
LL.M.—International Law;
  D.C.L., M.C.L.

Harvard University
Law School
Graduate Program in
  International Legal Studies
Cambridge, MA 02138
U.S.A.
S.J.D., LL.M.—Comparative Jurisprudence,
  Public International Law (among others)

University of Houston
Law Center
4800 Calhoun Road
Houston, TX 77004
U.S.A.
LL.M.—International Economic Law

Director of Graduate Programs
Howard University
School of Law
2900 Van Ness Street, N.W.
Washington, DC 20008
U.S.A.
M.C.J.

Graduate Studies Program
University of Illinois
College of Law
504 East Pennsylvania Avenue
Champaign, IL 61820
U.S.A.
LL.M.—International Law; M.C.L.

Illinois Institute of Technology
Chicago-Kent College of Law
77 South Wacker Drive
Chicago, IL 60606
U.S.A.
M.A.L.S./LL.M. (for non-United States law school
    graduates only)
(new law center address beginning January 1992:
565 West Adams Street
Chicago, IL 60606
U.S.A.)

Law School Admissions
Indiana University—Bloomington
School of Law
Third Street and Indiana Avenue
Bloomington, IN 47405
U.S.A.
M.C.L., LL.M.

University of Iowa
College of Law
Iowa City, IA 52242
U.S.A.
M.C.L.

Associate Director
Foreign Graduate Programs
University of Miami
School of Law
P.O. Box 248087
1311 Miller Drive
Coral Gables, FL 33124
U.S.A.
LL.M.—International Law; M.C.L.—Inter-American Law

Graduate Office
University of Michigan
Law School
Hutchins Hall
Ann Arbor, MI 48109-1215
U.S.A.
S.J.D., LL.M., M.C.L.

Committee on Admissions
New York University
School of Law
Vanderbilt Hall 419
40 Washington Square South
New York, NY 10012
U.S.A.
LL.M.—International Law, International Tax Law;
    M.C.J.—Inter-American Law

Northwestern University
School of Law
357 East Chicago Avenue
Chicago, IL 60611-3069
U.S.A.
LL.M.—International and Comparative Law (among others)

Notre Dame Law School
Notre Dame, IN 46556
U.S.A.
LL.M.—International Law; M.C.L. (course of study for both
    programs is normally completed at Notre Dame's
    London Law Centre in England)

Graduate Admissions Office
University of the Pacific
McGeorge School of Law
3200 Fifth Avenue
Sacramento, CA 95817
U.S.A.
LL.M.—Transnational Business Law

Southern Methodist University
School of Law
Dallas, TX 75275
U.S.A.
S.J.D., M.C.L., LL.M.—International Law

Temple University
School of Law
1719 North Broad Street
Philadelphia, PA 19122
U.S.A.
LL.M.—International Law

University of Texas
School of Law
727 East 26th Street
Austin, TX 78705
U.S.A.
M.C.J.

University of San Diego
School of Law
Alcalá Park
San Diego, CA 92110
U.S.A.
M.C.L., LL.M.—International Law

Assistant Director
Law School Admissions
Graduate Study Program
Tulane University
School of Law
Joseph Merrick Jones Hall
6801 Freret Street
New Orleans, LA 70118
U.S.A.
M.C.L., LL.M.—Admiralty Law

Director
Graduate Program
University of Virginia
School of Law
Charlottesville, VA 22901
U.S.A.
LL.M., S.J.D.—International Law

Graduate Admissions
University of Washington
School of Law
Condon Hall 316, JB-20
1100 N.E. Campus Parkway
Seattle, WA 98105
U.S.A.
Ph.D.—Comparative Law (with emphasis on East Asia);
    LL.M.—East Asian Law

Director, Graduate Programs
Yale Law School
127 Wall Street
Yale Station
Drawer 401A
New Haven, CT 06520
U.S.A.
J.S.D., LL.M.—law school teaching

INTRODUCTION
TO THE
ILSA CONFERENCE OF INTERNATIONAL LAW JOURNALS

The ILSA Conference of International Law Journals was started in the mid-1970's, with a small group of editors of student-edited international law journals gathering informally for ILSA (then known as ASILS)—sponsored workshops on managing a student-edited journal. In 1979, the ILSA Conference was formalized into an annual meeting of editors and staff members of student-run international law journals. The Conference meets for two days each spring, during the ILSA Annual Meeting (held in conjunction with the Annual Meeting of the American Society of International Law), and for one day each fall, during the ILSA Mid-Year Meeting (held in conjunction with the Annual Meeting of the American Branch of the International Law Association).

Each year a member journal volunteers to host the substantive portion of the annual Conference meetings. One member of the host journal is chosen as the Host Journal Representative. The Representative is responsible for planning the workshops on managing an international law journal and for seeking professional lecturers to speak on timely topics of international law. Workshops are sponsored by editors and staff of other member journals, who have expertise in various areas of managing an international law journal.

Pursuant to the ILSA Constitution, the school which hosts and publishes the *ILSA Journal of International Law* provides administrative support for the annual meetings of the Conference. One of the editors or staff members of the *ILSA Journal* is chosen to act as Assistant Conference Administrator for the Conference meetings and works closely with the Host Journal Representative.

In addition, the Host Journal Representative, the Editor-in-Chief of the *ILSA Journal* and the Executive Director of ILSA are charged with the overall coordination of Journal Conference activities during the year. While the *ILSA Journal* acts as a clearinghouse for student-written articles and publishes only student-written articles on timely issues of international law, the Host Journal of the conference also acts as a clearinghouse for all non-student-written articles which are submitted to the ILSA offices in Washington, D.C.

MEMBER JOURNALS OF THE
ILSA CONFERENCE OF INTERNATIONAL LAW JOURNALS

*Telephone numbers are provided for each entry. An asterisk (*)
denotes a school's general telephone number.*

ILSA Journal of International Law
Permanent administrative co-host of Conference
City University of New York (CUNY) Law School at
  Queen's College *(Host School 1990-1995)*
65-21 Main Street
Flushing, NY 11367
U.S.A.
1-718-575-4200*

**American University Journal of
  International Law & Policy**
American University
Washington College of Law
4400 Massachusetts Avenue, N.W.
Washington, DC 20016
U.S.A.
1-202-885-2696

**Arizona State Law School
  Journal of International Law**
Arizona State University
College of Law
Tempe, AZ 85287
U.S.A.
1-602-965-6181*

**Boston College International
  & Comparative Law Journal**
Boston College Law School
885 Centre Street
Newton, MA 02159
U.S.A.
1-617-552-8550*

**Boston College Third World
Law Journal**
Boston College Law School
885 Centre Street
Newton, MA 02159
U.S.A.
1-617-552-8550*

**Boston University International
Law Journal**
Boston University
School of Law
765 Commonwealth Avenue
Boston, MA 02115
U.S.A.
1-617-353-3157

Brooklyn Journal of International Law
Brooklyn Law School
250 Joralemon Street
Brooklyn, NY 11201
U.S.A.
1-718-780-7971

**California Western International
Law Journal**
California Western School of Law
350 Cedar Street
San Diego, CA 92101
U.S.A.
1-619-239-0391,* ext. 476

Canadian-American Law Journal
Gonzaga University
School of Law
East 702 Sharp Avenue
Box 3528
Spokane, WA 99220
U.S.A.
1-509-484-6481*

Canada-United States Law Journal
Case Western Reserve University
Law School
11075 East Boulevard
Cleveland, OH 44106
U.S.A.
1-216-368-3291

Case Western Reserve Journal
   of International Law
Case Western Reserve University
Law School
11075 East Boulevard
Cleveland, OH 44106
U.S.A.
1-216-368-3291

Columbia Human Rights Law
   Review
Columbia University
School of Law
435 West 116th Street
Box 54
New York, NY 10027
U.S.A.
1-212-854-2171*

Columbia Journal of
   Transnational Law
Columbia University
School of Law
435 West 116th Street
Box D-25
New York, NY 10027
U.S.A.
1-212-854-3742

Connecticut Journal of
   International Law
55 Elizabeth Street
University of Connecticut
School of Law
Hartford, CT 06105
U.S.A.
1-203-241-7680

**Cornell International
  Law Journal**
Cornell Law School
Myron Taylor Hall
Ithaca, NY 14853
U.S.A.
1-607-255-9666

**Denver Journal of International
  Law & Policy**
University of Denver
College of Law
7039 East 18th Avenue
Suite 235
Denver, CO 80220
U.S.A.
1-303-871-6166

**Dickinson Journal of
  International Law**
Dickinson School of Law
150 South College Street
Carlisle, PA 17013
U.S.A.
1-717-243-4611,* ext. 233

**Emory Journal of International
  Dispute Resolution**
Emory University School of Law
1722 North Decatur Road
Atlanta, GA 30322
U.S.A.
1-404-727-5774

Fletcher Forum
Fletcher School of Law
  and Diplomacy
Tufts University
Medford, MA 02155
U.S.A.
1-617-628-7010*

Florida International Law Journal
University of Florida
College of Law
Gainesville, FL 32611
U.S.A.
1-904-392-4980

Fordham International Law Journal
Fordham University
School of Law
Lincoln Center
140 West 62nd Street
New York, NY 10023-7477
U.S.A.
1-212-841-5175

**George Washington Journal of
    International Law and Economics**
George Washington University
National Law Center
2000 H Street, N.W.
Washington, DC 20052
U.S.A.
1-202-944-7164

**Georgetown International Environmental
    Law Review**
Georgetown University Law Center
600 New Jersey Avenue, N.W.
Washington, DC 20001
U.S.A.
1-202-662-9689

**Georgia Journal of International
    and Comparative Law**
University of Georgia
School of Law
Herty Drive
Athens, GA 30602
U.S.A.
1-404-542-7289

Harvard Human Rights Journal
Harvard University
Law School
Cambridge, MA 02138
U.S.A.
1-617-495-8318

Harvard International Law Journal
202 Hastings Hall
Harvard Law School
Cambridge, MA 02138
U.S.A.
1-617-495-3146

**Hastings International and
  Comparative Law Review**
University of California at
  San Francisco
Hastings College of Law
200 McAllister Street
Box H-170
San Francisco, CA 94102
U.S.A.
1-415-565-4730

Houston Journal of International Law
University of Houston Law Center
4800 Calhoun Road
Houston, TX 77004
U.S.A.
1-713-749-3774

Human Rights Annual
New York Law School
57 Worth Street
New York, NY 10013
U.S.A.
1-212-431-2112

Human Rights Quarterly
Urban Morgan Institute for
  Human Rights
University of Cincinnati
College of Law
Clifton and Calhoun Streets
Cincinnati, OH 45221
U.S.A.
1-513-556-0093; 1-513-556-0068

**Indiana International &
  Comparative Law Review**
Indiana University School of
  Law — Indianapolis
735 West New York Street
Indianapolis, IN 46202-5194
U.S.A.
1-317-274-1050

International Environmental Law Journal
University of Colorado
School of Law
Kitteridge Drive
Campus Box 401
Boulder, CO 80309
U.S.A.
1-303-492-2265

International Law Yearly
Willamette University
College of Law
250 Winter Street, S.E.
Salem, OR 97301
U.S.A.
1-503-370-6380*

International Legal Perspectives
Northwestern School of Law
Lewis and Clark College
10015 S.W. Terwilliger Boulevard
Portland, OR 97219
U.S.A.
1-503-244-1181*

International Tax & Business Lawyer
University of California at Berkeley
Boalt Hall School of Law
Berkeley, CA 94720
U.S.A.
1-415-642-9759

Journal of Air Law and Commerce
Southern Methodist University
School of Law
Dallas, TX 75275
U.S.A.
1-214-692-2570

Journal of Chinese Law
Columbia University
School of Law
435 West 116th Street
Box C-10
New York, NY 10027
U.S.A.
1-212-854-5350

Journal of Space Law
University of Mississippi
School of Law
University, MS 38677
U.S.A.
1-601-232-7361,* ext. 501 or ext. 503

Law and Policy in
  International Business
Georgetown University
Law Center
25 E Street, N.W.
Washington, DC 20001
U.S.A.
1-202-662-9000*

Leiden Journal of International Law
Rijksuniversiteit te Leiden
Faculteit der Reschtsgeleerdheid
Vakgroep Internationaal
Publiekrechtelijke Vakken
Hugo de Grootstraat 27
2311 XK Leiden
THE NETHERLANDS
31.71.27.27.27*

Loyola of Los Angeles International
  and Comparative Law Journal
Loyola Law School
1441 West Olympic Boulevard
P.O. Box 15019
Los Angeles, CA 90015-3980
U.S.A.
1-213-736-1405

Maryland Journal of International
  Law and Trade
University of Maryland
School of Law
500 West Baltimore Street
Baltimore, MD 21201
U.S.A.
1-301-328-6744

Michigan Journal of International Law
University of Michigan Law School
625 South State Street
Ann Arbor, MI 48109
U.S.A.
1-313-763-4597

New Europe Legal Studies
Benjamin N. Cardozo School of Law
Yeshiva University
55 Fifth Avenue
New York, NY 10003
U.S.A.
1-212-790-0200

New York Law School Journal of
  International and Comparative Law
New York Law School
57 Worth Street
New York, NY 10013
U.S.A.
1-212-431-2113

New York University Journal of
  International Law and Politics
New York University
School of Law
110 West Third Street
New York, NY 10012
U.S.A.
1-212-998-6520

North Carolina Journal of
  International and Commercial
  Regulation
University of North Carolina
School of Law
Ridge Road
Van Hecke-Wettach Hall
CB-3380
Chapel Hill, NC 27599-3380
U.S.A.
1-919-962-4402

Northwestern Journal of
  International Law and Business
Northwestern University
School of Law
357 East Chicago Avenue
Chicago, IL 60611-3069
U.S.A.
1-312-908-8742

Pace Yearbook of International Law
Pace University School of Law
78 North Broadway
White Plains, NY 10603
U.S.A.
1-914-422-4271

St. Thomas Law Forum
St. Thomas University School of Law
16400 N.W. 32nd Avenue
Miami, FL 33054
U.S.A.
1-305-623-2320*

Stanford Journal of International Law
Stanford Law School
Stanford, CA 94305
U.S.A.
1-415-723-1375

Suffolk Transnational Law Journal
Suffolk University Law School
41 Temple Street
Boston, MA 02114
U.S.A.
1-617-573-8610

Syracuse Journal of
   International Law and Commerce
Syracuse University
College of Law
E.I. White Hall
Syracuse, NY 13244
U.S.A.
1-315-443-2051

Temple International &
   Comparative Law Journal
Temple University
School of Law
1719 North Broad Street
Philadelphia, PA 19122
U.S.A.
1-215-787-8945

Texas International Law Journal
University of Texas
School of Law
727 East 26th Street
Austin, TX 78705
U.S.A.
1-512-471-5453

The Transnational Lawyer
University of the Pacific
McGeorge School of Law
3200 Fifth Avenue
Sacramento, CA 95817
U.S.A.
1-916-739-7133

University of Miami Inter-
   American Law Review
University of Miami
School of Law
P.O. Box 248087
1311 Miller Drive
Coral Gables, FL 33124
U.S.A.
1-305-284-5562

University of Pennsylvania
   Journal of International
   Business Law
University of Pennsylvania
Law School
3400 Chestnut Street
Philadelphia, PA 19104-6204
U.S.A.
1-215-898-7483*

Vanderbilt Journal of
   Transnational Law
Vanderbilt University
School of Law
21st Avenue South
Nashville, TN 37240
U.S.A.
1-615-322-2283

Virginia Journal of
   International Law
University of Virginia
School of Law
Charlottesville, VA 22901
U.S.A.
1-804-924-3237

**Wisconsin International
  Law Journal**
University of Wisconsin
Law School
975 Bascom Mall
Madison, WI 53706
U.S.A.
1-608-262-3877

Yale Journal of International Law
Yale Law School
Yale Station
Drawer 401A
New Haven, CT 06520-7397
U.S.A.
1-203-432-4884

NON-MEMBER JOURNALS

**Arizona Journal of International
  and Comparative Law**
University of Arizona
College of Law
Tucson, AZ 85721
U.S.A.
1-602-621-1373*

ELSA Law Review
ELSA International
c/o ELSA Zagreb
Gundulićeva 10
41000 Zagreb
YUGOSLAVIA
(or contact the ILSA offices in Washington, D.C., for
  further information)

**Touro Journal of Transnational
  Law**
Touro College
Jacob D. Fuchsberg Law Center
300 Nassau Road
Huntington, NY 11743
U.S.A.
1-516-421-2244*

UCLA Pacific Basin Law Journal
University of California at
  Los Angeles
School of Law
405 Hilgard Avenue
Los Angeles, CA 90024-1476
U.S.A.
1-213-206-6174

HOST JOURNALS OF THE
ILSA CONFERENCE OF INTERNATIONAL LAW JOURNALS

YEAR	JOURNAL
1979-80	*Lawyer of the Americas* (University of Miami) (now *University of Miami Inter-American Law Review*)
1980-81	*Brooklyn Journal of International Law*
1981-82	*George Washington Journal of International Law and Economics*
1982-83	*Denver Journal of International Law and Policy*
1983-84	*Houston Journal of International Law*
1984-85	*New York Law School Journal of International and Comparative Law*
1985-86	*Michigan Yearbook of International Legal Studies* (now *Michigan Journal of International Law*)
1986-87	*Houston Journal of International Law* (substantive co-host)
	Case Western Reserve Journal of International Law (administrative co-host)
1987-88	*Dickinson Journal of International Law* (substantive co-host)
	American University Journal of International Law and Policy (administrative co-host)
1988-89*	*Denver Journal of International Law and Policy*
1989-90	*Brooklyn Journal of International Law*
1990-91	*Brooklyn Journal of International Law*

* Since the 1988-89 Conference, the *ILSA Journal of International Law* has acted as permanent administrative co-host journal, pursuant to the ILSA Constitution.

FRANCIS O. DEAK AWARD

Each year the International Law Students Association, in conjunction with the American Society of International Law, presents the Francis O. Deak Award to the author of the best student-written article published in a student-edited international law journal. The author must be a student at the time of the writing and publication date of the article. A single entry is nominated each year by the editor-in-chief of each participating student-edited international law journal. The winning article is then selected by a panel of distinguished scholars and practitioners.

YEAR

1973   **Pearl, Allen R.** "Liberation of Capital in Japan." 13 *Harv. Int'l L.J.* 59 (1972).

1974   **Terr, Leonard B.** " 'The Distance Plus Joint Development Zone' Formula: A Proposal For the Speedy and Practical Resolution of the East China and Yellow Seas Continental Shelf Oil Controversy." 7 *Cornell Int'l L.J.* 49 (1973).

1975   **Marchisotto, Alan.** "The Protection of Art in Transnational Law." 7 *Vand. Int'l L.J.* 689 (1974).

1976   **Mooney, Thomas.** "A Delicate Balance: Equal Representation for Labor on German Corporate Boards." 16 *Harv. Int'l L.J.* 352 (1975).

1977   **Smith, Brian D.** "Canadian and Soviet Arctic Policy: An Icy Reception for the Law of the Sea?" 16 *VA. J. Int'l L.* 609 (1976).

1978   **Bukovac, Daniel.** "Securities Law Subject Matter Jurisdiction in Transnational Securities Fraud." 9 *N.Y.U. J. Int'l L. & Pol.* 113 (1977) (Tie).

      Wambold, Judson J. "Prohibiting Foreign Bribes: Criminal Sanctions for Corporate Payments Abroad." 10 *Cornell Int'l L.J.* 231 (1977) (Tie).

1979   **Smith, Ralph H.** "Beyond the Treaties: Limitations on Neutrality in the Panama Canal." 4 *Yale J. World Pub. Ord.* 1 (1977).

1980   **Golan, Jeffrey W.** "U.S. Technology Transfers to the Soviet Union and Protection of National Security." 11 *J.L. Pol'y Int'l Bus.* 1037 (1979).

1981   Rich, Frederic C. "Eurobond Practice: Sources of Law and the Threat of Unilateral National Regulation." 20 *VA. J. Int'l L.* 505 (1980).

1982   Pavlis, Paul A. "International Arbitration and the Inapplicability of the Act of State Doctrine." 14 *N.Y.U. J. Int'l L. & Pol.* 65 (1981).

1983   Maguire, J. Robert. "The Decolonization of Belize: Self Determination v. Territorial Integrity." 22 *VA. J. Int'l L.* 849 (1982).

1984   Cooper, David M. "Transborder Data Flow and the Protection of Privacy: The Harmonization of Data Protection Law." 8 *Fletcher Forum* 335 (1984).

1985   Nilles, Kathleen M. "Defining the Limits of Liability: A Legal and Political Analysis of the European Community Products Liability Directive." 25 *VA. J. Int'l L.* 729 (1985).

1986   Auwarter, Ellen C. "Compelled Waiver of Bank Secrecy in the Cayman Islands: Solution to International Tax Evasion or Threat to Sovereignty of Nations?" 9 *Fordham Int'l L. J.* 680 (1986).

1987   Willems, John S. "From Treblinka to the Killing Fields: Excluding Persecutors from the Definition of 'Refugee'." 27 *VA. J. Int'l L.* 823 (1987).

1988   Leh, Christopher M. "Remedying Foreign Repression Through U.S. Courts: *Forti v. Suarez-Mason* and the Recognition of Torture, Summary Execution, Prolonged Aribtrary Detention and Causing Disappearance as Cognizable Claims Under the Alien Tort Claims Act." 20 *N.Y.U. J. Int'l L. & Pol.* 405 (1988).

1989   Galfand, Edward. "Heeding the Call for a Predictable Rule of Origin." 11 *U. PA. J. Int'l Bus. L.* 469 (1989).

THE *ILSA JOURNAL OF INTERNATIONAL LAW*

In 1977, the Association, under the direction of then ASILS Executive Secretary Kenneth Klein, began publishing the *ILSA Journal of International Law* (formerly the *ASILS International Law Journal*). In the late 1970's the *ILSA Journal* was edited and published at the ILSA office in Washington, D.C. The Executive Director of ILSA (then known as the ASILS Executive Secretary) served as Editor-in-Chief, and students from law schools across the United States filled the other editorial positions. Pamela M. Young, the Assistant Jessup Administrator, served as Administrative Assistant.

In the fall of 1980, the system of utilizing a host school for the *ILSA Journal* was instituted. American University and the University of Denver co-hosted the publication of the Journal and received editorial assistance from a group of other law schools. In 1982, full editorial and publication duties were transferred to a single host school.

Since 1984, the *ILSA Journal* has been hosted in five-year cycles. The Benjamin N. Cardozo School of Law was the first school to host the *ILSA Journal* on such a basis. After an additional year of transition for the *ILSA Journal* at Cardozo, the City University of New York (CUNY) Law School at Queens College assumed the next five-year cycle in the fall of 1990. Pursuant to the ILSA Constitution, proposals from schools interested in hosting the *ILSA Journal* are solicited during the third year of each hosting cycle.

The *ILSA Journal* is published once each year. Each issue is devoted exclusively to articles written by ILSA student members on timely subjects of international and comparative law. Each volume also includes Jessup Competition materials from the corresponding year.

In addition to acting as a forum for student-authored articles, the *ILSA Journal* provides a unique opportunity for schools who wish to publish their own international law journal to develop an editorial infrastructure while publishing the *ILSA Journal*. The editorial board of the Host School is responsible for editing and publishing the *ILSA Journal*, as well as providing administrative assistance to the ILSA Conference of International Law Journals. The board also presents the annual Dean Rusk Award to the author of the best-written article published in the *ILSA Journal* that year. The ILSA offices administer the subscriptions and distribution of the *ILSA Journal*.

For more information on publishing an article in the *ILSA Journal of International Law*, or hosting the *ILSA Journal*, please contact the ILSA offices in Washington, D.C.

HOST SCHOOLS OF THE *ILSA JOURNAL*
1976-1995

* — not a law school

Volume	Years	Host School(s)
I	1976-77	Editorial board consisting of students from the following schools: American University, University of Virginia, University of Pennsylvania, Stanford University, University of South Carolina, Georgetown University, University of Georgia, International Law School (now George Mason University), Wellesley College*, the University of Chicago and the Free University of Brussels.
II	1977-78	Editorial board consisting of students from the following schools: International Law School (now George Mason University), California Western, Potomac School of Law, University of Michigan, Georgetown University and the Catholic University of America.
III	1978-79	Editorial board consisting of students from the following schools: Ohio State University, University of Georgia, George Mason University, University of San Diego, Georgetown University, Cumberland School of Law, Capital University and the Catholic University of America.
IV	1979-80	Editorial board consisting of students from the following schools: Albany Law School, University of Puget Sound, Northwestern University, University of Kentucky, American University, University of San Diego and Boston College Law School.

Volume	Years	Host School(s)
V	1980-81	American University and University of Denver, with assistance from the University of California at Berkeley, Albany Law School, Stanford University, Southwestern University, George Washington University and Ohio State University
VI	1981-82	Willamette University, with assistance from University of Puget Sound and Washington and Lee University
VII	1982-83	University of Iowa
VIII	1983-84	DePaul University
IX-XIV	1984-90	Cardozo Law School, Yeshiva University
XV-XIX	1990-95	City University of New York (CUNY) Law School at Queen's College

INTRODUCTION
TO THE
PHILIP C. JESSUP INTERNATIONAL LAW
MOOT COURT COMPETITION

The Philip C. Jessup International Law Moot Court Competition, cosponsored each year by the International Law Students Association and the American Society of International Law, is the largest competition of its kind in the world. As the only worldwide moot court competition in international law, the Jessup annually involves approximately 250 universities in 40 countries on six continents. In its more than thirty-year history, over 437 universities in 71 countries have been involved in the Competition at one time or another. There are now over 30,000 former Jessup participants, judges and supporters worldwide, and the number grows by over 1,000 each year.

This section of the *Guide* contains the history of the Jessup Competition and a photograph of the World Championship Jessup Cup. For a detailed year-by-year review of Jessup Competition data from the first round of the Jessup in 1960 to the latest World Championship Jessup Cup Round, please refer to the annually updated *Philip C. Jessup International Law Moot Court Competition Reporter*, available through the ILSA offices in Washington, D.C. The *Reporter* lists, cross-referenced by year and/or subject area, the following information (*inter alia*): the participation and performance of all individual schools (and their countries) involved in all levels of the Competition worldwide; the location, rankings and official results of the semifinal and final rounds of the Competition; the recipients of the Best Oralist and Best Memorial Awards; and, the Jessup Problem authors, final round judges and international administrators of the Competition. For the full texts of Jessup Problems, Judges' Memoranda, Official Rules, and Best Memorials from the Competition, as well as a more general summary of each year's Jessup Competition results, please refer to the appropriate volumes of the *Philip C. Jessup International Law Moot Court Competition Compendium*, available in many law libraries around the globe.

We would like to thank all those worldwide who have contributed their time, effort and money to the Jessup Competition over the years. Without you, it would not have been possible. We would also like to encourage anyone who is interested to become involved in the Friends of the Jessup support groups forming at the Jessup headquarters in Washington, D.C., and around the world. It is your support (both in judging and in administration), your encouragement, and your contributions that will define the future of the Jessup Competition, and, indeed, the development of international law, in the years to come.

THE HISTORY
OF THE
PHILIP C. JESSUP INTERNATIONAL LAW
MOOT COURT COMPETITION

The Jessup Competition was founded in the spring of 1959 by a group of international law students from Harvard University, Columbia University and the University of Virginia, assembled at the Annual Meeting of the American Society of International Law in Washington, D.C. Encouraged by their international law professors and motivated by the pressing events of world decolonization, space exploration and the Cold War, the students began to organize various cooperative activities to promote international legal education at their schools. Among these activities was an international law moot court in which oral and written pleadings would be presented on issues of international law in hypothetical cases before the International Court of Justice in the Hague.

Originally named the "International Law Moot," the Jessup Competition held its first round at Harvard University on 3 May 1960. The round, held among Harvard Law students, involved a team of two American law students, Thomas J. Farer and William D. Zabel, and a team of two foreign LL.M. students, Ivan L. Head of Canada and Bernard H. Clark of New Zealand, pleading the hypothetical "Cuban Agrarian Reform Case." This first Jessup case was written by then Assistant Professor Stephen M. Schwebel of Harvard Law School, now Judge of the International Court of Justice. Presiding over the round were Milton Katz, as President, and Stephen M. Schwebel and Roger Fisher, as Justices.

The Second Annual Jessup Competition, the first inter-school Jessup Competition, was held at Columbia University in 1961 with the support of Professor Wolfgang G. Friedmann of Columbia Law School. Harvard, Yale and Columbia Universities participated. In 1962, at the encouragement of then Professor Richard R. Baxter of Harvard Law School, later Judge of the International Court of Justice, and other members of the American Society of International Law, the Jessup Competition was held for the first time at the Annual Meeting of the American Society of International Law. The International Semifinal and Final rounds of the Competition have been held during the Annual Meeting of the ASIL ever since. Duke University, Columbia University, and the first Canadian team

227

to participate in the Competition, Osgoode Hall Law School of York University, were the three teams participating in this third Annual Jessup Competition.

During the 1962 ASIL meeting, law student delegates from Harvard, Columbia, Yale, Virginia and Duke Universities held a special meeting to discuss the future of the Jessup Competition and other student international law activities. In recognition of the growing interest in the International Law Moot and other student activities, and the need to coordinate these activities between the international law student groups of the various law schools, the delegates assembled founded the Association of Student International Law Societies (ASILS), an umbrella organization entrusted with the administration of the moot competition as well as other cooperative student activities. This organization has become today's International Law Students Association (ILSA).

For the Fourth Annual Jessup Competition in 1962-63, the Competition expanded to include eight United States teams which competed in two regionals. The winning teams from these two regionals advanced to the final round of the Competition at the Annual Meeting of the American Society of International Law, where, for the first time, an overall winner of the Competition was declared. This system of regionals and semifinals proved highly successful and has remained in place ever since. Also at the 1963 Annual Meeting, after consultation with the members of the American Society of International Law, the students of the newly-formed ASILS officially named the Competition in honor of Judge Philip C. Jessup of the International Court of Justice.

Now known as the "Philip C. Jessup International Law Moot Court Competition," the Competition experienced great success during the remaining years of the 1960's, expanding from eight teams completing participation in 1963, to thirty-five teams in 1969. This success, however, brought with it great difficulties for the student-led administrative structure that had been in place since 1962. In the late 1960's, recognizing the ever-increasing and often unrealistic burden that was being placed on the ASILS student officer assigned to administer the Competition each year (as well as the need for a central administrative headquarters for the Competition), the then Executive Director of the American Society of International Law, Stephen M. Schwebel, in cooperation with the students of the ASILS, sought to create a full-time fellowship position for the administrator of the Competition. This fellowship position was to be located at Tillar House, home of the American Society of

International Law, in Washington, D.C., and would be filled by a recent law graduate specializing in international law.

After a number of efforts in support of the idea by both the American Society of International Law and the ASILS, the fellowship became a reality with the pledge of a three-year grant by the Henry Luce Foundation beginning in 1969. With the establishment of the fellowship, the American Society of the International Law became the official cosponsor of the Jessup Competition and the Host Professional Organization of the ASILS. The survival, as well as the professional and fair administration of the Jessup Competition, was, for the first time, assured.

In addition to supporting the fellowship, the American Society of International Law also sought at this time to internationalize the Competition beyond North America by soliciting funds from the United States Department of State to support the participation of teams from other continents. The first team to receive such support, and the first European team to participate in the Jessup Competition, was the School of Law and Economics of Paris, France, which participated in the 1969 Competition. With the continued support of the U.S. Department of State in the early 1970's, international participation in the Competition grew to include teams from Argentina, Ethiopia, Liberia, Nigeria, the United Kingdom, and Zambia.

In 1972, the Competition was split into two divisions—the "National Division" for teams from the United States (then numbering 53), and the "International Division" for teams representing other countries (then numbering 8). The winner from each division then met in the World Championship Jessup Cup Round. This structure, originally designed to guarantee an international final round and to help balance a perceived unequal "competitiveness" among teams, remained until 1987, when the number and "competitiveness" of teams in the International Division had become roughly comparable to that of the National Division. In addition, the segregated divisions were increasingly creating an artificial national bias and a restraint on the international experience of the participants.

In 1988, the divisions were eliminated and the competition was unified under a newly integrated structure. This new structure, which includes expanded international final rounds, now assures equal treatment within an international environment for all participating countries, as well as an international World Championship Jessup Cup Round. In order to provide balance for the Competition around the world under the new structure, and to give each team an equal opportunity to advance to the semifinals, the advancement rule of "one team per country or one team for every group of ten teams participating nationally" was adopted, prior to the 1989 Competition.

During the 1970's, the Jessup Competition experienced an incredible four-fold increase in the number of teams completing participation each year, from 40 in 1970 to 156 in 1979. In addition, the number of countries represented at the semifinals jumped from 5 in 1970 to 23 in 1979. The number of annual regional competitions (of varying sizes) also grew from 7 in 1970 to 17 in 1979. Australia, Canada, the Federal Republic of Germany, India, the Netherlands, Nigeria, Pakistan and the United Kingdom all joined the United States in hosting regional Jessup competitions in the 1970's.

This growth in the Jessup Competition, however, was accompanied by continued financial uncertainty. Upon completion of the Luce Foundation grant in 1973, a combination of emergency funds was obtained from the American Society of International Law, the Rockefeller Foundation, and the U.S. Government, in order to keep the Jessup Fellowship alive until 1978, when the Charles A. Dana Foundation stepped in with a seven-year commitment to support the fellowship. In addition to concern for the fellowship, the general expenses of the Jessup also increased during this period, reflecting the growth of the Competition. A part-time administrative assistant was added and a small Jessup Endowment was established in 1975. Registration fees for teams were slightly increased and U.S. Government support for teams from outside of North America continued.

The 1980's proved to be a highly successful, yet very difficult, decade for the Jessup Competition. Although the reputation and quality of the Competition, as well as its level of participation, enjoyed their highest levels ever, financial uncertainties and the lack of staff continued to plague the administration of the Jessup.

Teams completing participation in the Jessup Competition each year increased 34% between 1980 and 1987, from 176 to 236 schools. From 1980 to 1988, countries represented at the International Semifinals increased 26%, from 23 to 29 countries, after a drop of up to six countries in the early 1980's due to the suspension of regular U.S. Government support for teams from outside of North America. During the 1980's, U.S. Government support continued on a sporadic basis, and only for teams from developing countries. Thus, many teams around the world initiated their own private fundraising efforts. Regional competitions during this period grew from 19 in 1980 to a high of 24 in 1987, with Belgium, Ireland, Japan, Mexico, New Zealand, the Philippines, Spain and Taiwan hosting their first Jessup regionals in the 1980's.

As stated earlier, financial difficulties continued to plague the Competition in the 1980's. The Dana Foundation grant in support of the Jessup Fellowship concluded at the end of 1985, leaving the Competition with no support funds for the fellowship at a time when the Competition had grown to over five times the size it had been when the fellowship was created in 1969. With help from the Exxon Corporation, the ASILS and the American Society of International Law were able to complete the administration of the 1986 Jessup Competition; but the survival of the Competition, without forthcoming outside support, was again in doubt.

From 1986 to 1989, with a combination of staff cuts, direct support from the American Society of International Law, a large increase in registration fees, and a series of revenue-generating projects, the students of the newly-constituted International Law Students Association (ILSA) and the members of the American Society of International Law continued to support the fellowship and to seek more financial self-sufficiency for the Jessup Competition. Important additions to their efforts included the creation of the "Friends of the Jessup" support group for the Competition, made up of former participants, judges and supporters of the Jessup worldwide, and the pledge of the American Bar Association (in following sister associations around the world which support their national Jessup competitions) to provide financial and judging assistance for the U.S. national regionals of the Jessup. These efforts have led to some success, but long-term solutions to staffing and funding problems at the Jessup office and financial support for teams worldwide must be found.

As we enter the 1990's, the value and impact of the Jessup Competition have never been greater. From Japan to Hungary, the United States to Papua New Guinea, former Jessup participants, as well as judges, sharing their common Jessup experiences, are now entering foreign, finance, and justice ministries in increasing numbers. They can also be found in the world's finest law firms, corporations, universities, parliaments and international organizations. Requests from governments for written materials submitted to the Jessup Competition increase each year, along with inquiries from new schools wishing to participate in the Competition. At regional competitions around the globe (in, *inter alia*, Pondicherry,

India; the Hague, the Netherlands; Tokyo, Japan; and, Los Angeles, California) and at the International Semifinals, Jessup participants worldwide continue to contribute their efforts to the development of international legal education, as well as international law itself.

The World Championship Jessup Cup. *(photo courtesy of the University of British Columbia, Canada)*

INTRODUCTION
TO THE
ILSA CONGRESS OF INTERNATIONAL LAW SOCIETIES

The ILSA Congress of International Law Societies is the representative assembly of the International Law Students Association. It consists of all ILSA member international law societies and an at-large membership representative elected by individual members of ILSA who are without an ILSA member society at their school. The member societies and the at-large membership representative each receive one vote in the Congress. In cooperation with the ILSA Executive Committee, the ILSA Congress formulates overall Association policy, including its Constitution and Bylaws.* The ILSA Executive Committee, consisting of all ILSA officers, manages the Association's affairs, reports to the Congress, and acts as liaison with ILSA's Host Professional Organization.

The ILSA Congress meets twice each year, for a fall session and a spring session. Regional meetings may also be organized by member societies. The fall session of the Congress is held in November at ILSA'a Mid-Year Meeting in New York, which takes place in conjunction with the Annual Meeting of the American Branch of the International Law Association. The spring session of the Congress is held at ILSA's Annual Meeting in April, usually in Washington, D.C. This meeting is held in conjunction with the Annual Meeting of the American Society of International Law, ILSA's Host Professional Organization. At each spring session, the ILSA Congress elects a Chair and Vice-Chair of the Congress, who sit on ILSA's Executive Committee. The Chair of the Congress, who presides over all Congress sessions, is the chief student officer of ILSA and is empowered to appoint special working groups and an advisory cabinet of regional coordinators for society activities. The Vice-Chair of the Congress assists both the Chair and the Executive Director of ILSA in their activities.

Acting as a forum for information exchange between member societies, as well as individual members, the ILSA Congress initiates and coordinates ILSA's worldwide communications, education and career activities in support of its member societies and

---

* Copies of the ILSA Constitution and Bylaws may be obtained through the ILSA offices in Washington, D.C.

individuals. These activities include, *inter alia*, workshops on running an international law society, panel discussions on opportunities in international law, inter-society cooperation on projects and scheduling of events, support for international law curricula and programs on campuses (including the Jessup Competition and international law journal activities), compilation of professional speakers lists for member societies, and information and contributions for the *ILSA Newsletter*.

MEMBER SCHOOLS OF THE INTERNATIONAL LAW STUDENTS ASSOCIATION

The following is a list of ILSA member societies:

AUSTRALASIA

Australia

Australian National University—International Law Students Association
Bond University, Queensland, Australia—Bond University International Law Students Association
University of Melbourne—International Law Society
Monash University—Law Student's Society
University of New South Wales—Julius Stone Society of International Law
Queensland University of Technology—International Law Students Association
University of Sydney—International Law Society
University of Tasmania—International Law Society
University of Western Australia—Blackstone Society

New Zealand

Auckland University—Law Students Society

Singapore

National University of Singapore—Law Club

ASIA

Hong Kong

City Polytechnic of Hong Kong—International Law Society

Japan

Kyoto University—International Law Society
Osaka City University—International Law Studies Group
Rikkyo (St. Paul's) University—International Law Students Association
University of Tokyo—Society for International Law Students
Waseda University—International Law Society

EUROPE

Austria

Universität zu Wien—International Law Society

Bulgaria

Sofia University—International Law Society

Germany

Institut für Völkerrecht der Universität Bonn—International Law
Society

Ireland

The Law Students' Debating Society of Ireland, King's Inn—
International Law Society

The Netherlands

Rijksuniversiteit te Leiden—Telders Society of International Law
Rijksuniversiteit te Utrecht—International Law Society

Switzerland

The Graduate Institute of International Studies (in cooperation
with the Université de Genève)—Law Committee

United Kingdom

Aberdeen University—Law Society
University of Birmingham—International Law Students
Association
University of Hull—International Law Society
Leicester Polytechnic School of Law—Students Law Society
University of Southampton—Law Faculty Students Society
University of Strathclyde—Law Society
University of Warwick—Law Society

NORTH AMERICA

Canada

Queen's University—International Law Society
University of New Brunswick—International Law Society

United States

University of Akron, C. Blake McDowell Law Center—
International Law Society

University of Alabama School of Law—International Law Society
Albany Law School, Union University—International Law Society
American University, Washington College of Law—International
  Law Society
Arizona State University College of Law—International Law
  Society
University of Baltimore School of Law—International Law
  Society
Baylor University School of Law—International Law Society
Boston College Law School—International Law Society
Boston University School of Law—International Law Society
University of Bridgeport School of Law—International Law
  Society
Brigham Young University, J. Reuben Clark Law School—
  J. Reuben Clark International and Comparative Law Society
Brooklyn Law School—International Law Society
University of California at Berkeley School of Law (Boalt Hall)—
  International Law Society
University of California at Davis School of Law—International
  Law Society
University of California at Los Angeles—International Law
  Society
University of California at San Francisco, Hastings College of
  Law—Dickinson Society of International Law
California Western School of Law—International Law Society
Capital University Law School—International Law Society
Case Western Reserve University Law School—Society of
  International Law Students
Catholic University of America School of Law—International
  Law Society
University of Cincinnati College of Law—John B. Hollister
  Society of International Law
City University of New York (CUNY) Law School at Queens
  College—International Law Society
Cleveland State University, Cleveland-Marshall College of Law—
  International Law Society
University of Colorado School of Law—Nicholas B. Doman
  International Law Society
Columbia University School of Law—Columbia Society of
  International Law
University of Connecticut School of Law—Adlai E. Stevenson
  Society of International Law

Thomas M. Cooley Law School—International Law Society
Cornell Law School—Herbert W. Briggs Society of International Law
Creighton University School of Law—International Law Society
Cumberland School of Law of Samford University—International Law Society
University of Dayton School of Law—International Law Society
University of Denver College of Law—International Law Society
DePaul University College of Law—International Law Society
Detroit College of Law—International Law Society
University of Detroit School of Law—International Law Students Association
Dickinson School of Law—International Law Society
Duke University School of Law—International Law Society
Duquesne University School of Law—International Law Society
Emory University School of Law—International Law Society
Fletcher School of Law and Diplomacy—Leo Gross International Law Society
University of Florida College of Law—International Law Society
Fordham University School of Law—Fordham International Law Society
Franklin Pierce Law Center—International Law Society
George Mason University School of Law—International Law Society
George Washington University National Law Center—International Law Society
Georgetown University Law Center—James Brown Scott Society of International Law
University of Georgia School of Law—Georgia Society of International and Comparative Law
Georgia State University College of Law—International and Comparative Law Society
Golden Gate University School of Law—International Law Society
Gonzaga University School of Law—International Law Society
Hamline University School of Law—International Law Society
Harvard University Law School—International Law Society
University of Hawaii, William S. Richardson School of Law—International Law Students Association/Pacific-Asian Legal Studies Students Organization (PALSSO)
Hofstra University School of Law—International Law Society
University of Houston Law Center—International Law Society

Howard University School of Law — William S. Thompson
  International Law Society
University of Idaho College of Law — International Law Society
University of Illinois College of Law — International Law Society
Illinois Institute of Technology, Chicago-Kent College of Law —
  Chancellor Kent International Law Society
Indiana University at Bloomington School of Law — Indiana
  University International Law Association
Indiana University School of Law, Indianapolis — Wendell L.
  Wilke Society of International Law
University of Iowa College of Law — Society of International Law
  and Affairs
The Johns Hopkins University, School of Advanced International
  Studies (SAIS) — International Law Society
University of Kansas School of Law — International Law Society
University of Kentucky College of Law — International Law
  Society
Lewis and Clark College, Northwestern School of Law —
  International Law Society
University of Louisville School of Law — International Law
  Society
Lousiana State University Law Center — International Law
  Society
Loyola University School of Law, Chicago — International Law
  Society
Loyola University School of Law, New Orleans — International
  Law Society
Loyola Law School at Los Angeles — International Law Society
University of Maine School of Law — International Law Society
Marquette University Law School — International Law Society
The John Marshall Law School — John Marshall International
  Law Society
University of Maryland School of Law — International Law
  Society
Memphis State University, Cecil C. Humphreys School of Law —
  International Law Society
University of Miami School of Law — International Law Society
University of Michigan Law School — International Law Society
University of Minnesota Law School — International and
  Comparative Law Society
University of Mississippi School of Law — Lamar Society of
  International Law

William Mitchell College of Law—International Law Society

New England School of Law—International Law Society

University of New Mexico School of Law—Association of
International Law Students

State University of New York (SUNY) at Buffalo School of
Law—SUNY-Buffalo International Law Society

New York Law School—International Law Society

New York University School of Law—International Law Society

University of North Carolina School of Law—University of North
Carolina-Chapel Hill International Law Society

Northern Illinois University College of Law—Northern Illinois
International Law Society

Northern Kentucky University, Salmon P. Chase College of
Law—International Law Society

Northwestern University School of Law—International Law
Society

Notre Dame Law School—International Law Society

Nova University Center for the Study of Law—International
Law Society

Ohio Northern University, Pettit College of Law—Ohio Northern
University International Law Society

Ohio State University College of Law—International Law Society

Oklahoma City University School of Law—Oklahoma City
University International Law Students Association

University of Oklahoma Law Center—International Law Society

University of Oregon School of Law—International Law Students
Association

Pace University School of Law—International Law Society

University of the Pacific, McGeorge School of Law—Pacific
International Law Society

University of Pennsylvania Law School—International Law
Society

Pepperdine University School of Law—International Law Society

University of Pittsburgh School of Law—International Law
Society

University of Puget Sound School of Law—International Law
Society

Rutgers, The State University of New Jersey School of Law,
Camden—Francis Deak International Law Society

Rutgers, The State University of New Jersey, S.I. Newhouse
Center for Law & Justice, Newark—Rutgers International
Law Society

St. John's University School of Law—Society of International
and Comparative Law

St. Louis University School of Law—International Law Society

St. Mary's University of San Antonio School of Law—
International Law Association

St. Thomas University School of Law—St. Thomas International
Law Society

University of San Diego School of Law—International Law
Society

University of San Francisco School of Law—University of San
Francisco International Law Society

Santa Clara University School of Law—International Law
Society

Seton Hall University School of Law—International Law Society

University of South Carolina School of Law—International Law
Society

South Texas College of Law—South Texas College of Law
International Law Students Association

University of Southern California Law Center—University of
Southern California International Law Society

Southern Illinois University School of Law—Donald F. McHenry
International Law Society

Southern Methodist University School of Law—International
Law Society

Southwestern University School of Law—International Law
Society

Stanford Law School—International Law Society

Suffolk University College of Law—International Law Society

Syracuse University College of Law—International Law Society

Temple University School of Law—Temple University
International Law Society

The University of Texas School of Law—International Law
Society

Texas Tech University School of Law—International Law Society

University of Toledo College of Law—Toledo International Law
Society

Tulane University School of Law—Eberhard P. Deutsch
International Law Society

The University of Tulsa College of Law—International Law
Society

Valparaiso University School of Law—International Law Society

Vanderbilt University School of Law—International Law Society

Villanova University School of Law—Villanova Law School
  International Law Society
University of Virginia School of Law—John Bassett Moore
  Society of International Law
Wake Forest University School of Law—International Law
  Society
Washburn University School of Law—International Law Society
Washington and Lee University School of Law—International
  Law Society
University of Washington School of Law—University of
  Washington International Law Society
Washington University School of Law—International Law
  Society
Wayne State University Law School—International Law Society
West Virginia University College of Law—International Law
  Society
Western New England College School of Law—International Law
  Society
Western State University School of Law, Fullerton—
  International Law Society
Western State University School of Law, San Diego—
  International Law Society
Whittier College School of Law—Whittier International Law
  Society
Widener University School of Law, Wilmington—International
  Law Society
Willamette University College of Law—International Law
  Society
College of William and Mary, Marshall-Wythe School of Law—
  International Law Society
University of Wisconsin Law School—Wisconsin International
  Law Society
Yale Law School—Yale International Law Association
Yeshiva University, Benjamin N. Cardozo School of Law—
  International Law Society

SOUTH AMERICA

Chile

Instituto de Estudios Internacionales de la Universidad de
  Chile—Sociedad Estudiantil de Derecho Internacional

Colombia

Universidad de los Andes—International Law Society

Costa Rica

Universidad de Costa Rica—Sociedad de Derecho Internacional

Venezuela

Universidad Católica, Andres Bello—Sociedad de Derecho
Internacional

OTHER

ILSA Society-At-Large

(Individual ILSA Members without a member society)

INTERNATIONAL LAW STUDENTS ASSOCIATION (ILSA)
ORGANIZATIONAL FLOW CHART

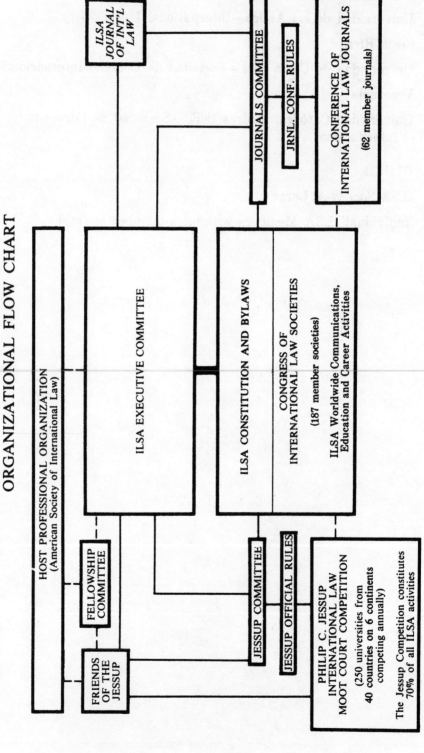

ILSA JOURNAL OF INT'L LAW

JOURNALS COMMITTEE

JRNL. CONF. RULES

CONFERENCE OF INTERNATIONAL LAW JOURNALS
(62 member journals)

HOST PROFESSIONAL ORGANIZATION
(American Society of International Law)

ILSA EXECUTIVE COMMITTEE

ILSA CONSTITUTION AND BYLAWS

CONGRESS OF INTERNATIONAL LAW SOCIETIES
(187 member societies)

ILSA Worldwide Communications, Education and Career Activities

FELLOWSHIP COMMITTEE

FRIENDS OF THE JESSUP

JESSUP COMMITTEE

JESSUP OFFICIAL RULES

PHILIP C. JESSUP INTERNATIONAL LAW MOOT COURT COMPETITION
(250 universities from 40 countries on 6 continents competing annually)

The Jessup Competition constitutes 70% of all ILSA activities

Join*—

THE AMERICAN SOCIETY OF INTERNATIONAL LAW

Society membership includes:

- four issues each year of the most distinguished journal in the field, *THE AMERICAN JOURNAL OF INTERNATIONAL LAW.*

- the Society's *NEWSLETTER.*

- the opportunity to buy other Society publications at reduced prices, such as the valuable bimonthly documentary, *INTERNATIONAL LEGAL MATERIALS*, the *PROCEEDINGS* of the Society's Annual Meeting, and books published under Society auspices.

- the opportunity to participate in significant Society-sponsored meetings (the Annual Meeting, regional meetings, study panels).

- occasion to join with others in contributing to the development of international law through the Society's wide-ranging studies and publications.

call or write:

MEMBERSHIP DIRECTOR
AMERICAN SOCIETY OF INTERNATIONAL LAW
2223 MASSACHUSETTS AVENUE, N.W.
WASHINGTON, D.C. 20008-2864 U.S.A.
Tel. 1-202-265-4313
FAX: 1-202-797-7133

* Be sure to inquire about the special membership offer available for ILSA members.

American Journal of International Law

As the Information Age brings the far corners of the globe ever closer together, professionals in many fields must be able to follow developments in international law. The *American Journal of International Law* analyzes the latest trends for scholars, diplomats, practicing attorneys, and professionals in international law, economics, trade, and foreign affairs. AJIL provides articles and editorials, comments on the contemporary practice of the U.S. relating to international law, summaries of international court decisions, discussion of current developments, and reviews of books published in many languages on issues ranging from international trade to human rights.

Published continuously by the American Society of International Law since 1907, AJIL now appears in January, April, July, and October.

Advertising space is available.

Address inquiries to:

American Journal of International Law
2223 Massachusetts Avenue, N.W.
Washington, D.C. 20008-2864 U.S.A.

International Law Students Association

ILSA JOURNAL OF INTERNATIONAL LAW*

International Law Students Association

The **ILSA Journal of International Law** is the only entirely student-written periodical in the international law field. Offering the finest work by students throughout the world, it is in effect a companion to the **American Journal of International Law.**

The Journal's most distinguished feature is the annual materials of the **Philip C. Jessup International Law Moot Court Competition,** including the Baxter Award-winning memorials.

Back issues are also available.

Please address orders to:

ILSA
2223 Massachusetts Avenue, N.W.
Washington, D.C. 20008-2864 U.S.A.
Tel. 1-202-265-4375
FAX: 1-202-797-7133

ILSA is affiliated with
The American Society of International Law

*Formerly known as ASILS International Law Journal

THE PHILIP C. JESSUP
INTERNATIONAL LAW
MOOT COURT COMPETITION
COMPENDIUM

Sponsored by the
International Law Students Association
and the
American Society of International Law

Jessup materials since 1960

For over thirty years, the Jessup Competition has provided foreign and domestic law school students with the unique opportunity to argue complex and timely questions of international law. Teams from over 250 law schools in some 40 countries participate annually.

This compilation draws together in one place for the first time, the Problems, the Judge's Briefs, the Rules and leading written Memorials which comprise the Philip C. Jessup International Law Moot Court Competition. Its aim is to promote international peace and understanding.

This work will enhance the law student's ability to grasp the practical side of the law by presenting award-winning responses to hypothetical problems.

Students wishing to enter the Jessup Competition in the future will find this work a valuable reference tool to prepare themselves for the Competition.

The William S. Hein & Co., Inc., sincerely believes this Compendium will be a valuable asset to your international collection.

Please note that 70% of the winners from past competitions have this set and have found it to be an invaluable aid in preparing them for upcoming competitions.

WILLIAM S. HEIN & CO., INC.
LAW PUBLISHER • MICROPUBLISHER • SUBSCRIPTION AGENT
NEW AND USED LAW BOOKS

1285 MAIN STREET, BUFFALO, N.Y. 14209 U.S.A.
1-716-882-2600 • TOLL FREE, 1-800-828-7571
MANHATTAN, 1-212-283-3528

International Law Students Association

For information on obtaining additional copies of the *ILSA Guide to Education and Career Development in International Law*, please contact the ILSA offices in Washington, D.C. ILSA also offers for sale videotapes, including World Championship Jessup Cup Round tapes (from 1987 to present) and tapes on research in, and sources of, international law. Also available are copies of the *Philip C. Jessup International Law Moot Court Competition Reporter* and ILSA and Jessup T-shirts/sweatshirts. Please contact the ILSA offices for more information.

ILSA
2223 Massachusetts Avenue, N.W.
Washington, D.C. 20008-2864 U.S.A.
Tel.   1-202-265-4375
FAX: 1-202-797-7133